LIBERATED LOVE

He [God] was as underhand as a lover, taking advantage of a passing mood.

Graham Greene

LIBERATED LOVE

Chester A. Pennington

A Pilgrim Press Book
from
United Church Press
Philadelphia

Copyright © 1972 United Church Press

The quotation preceding the title page (re-
peated on page 91) is from *The End of the
Affair* by Graham Greene. Copyright 1951 by
Graham Greene. Reprinted by permission of
The Viking Press, Inc.

Library of Congress Cataloging in Publication Data

Pennington, Chester A.
  Liberated love.

  "A Pilgrim Press book."
  Includes bibliographical references.
  1. Love. 2. Sex and religion. 3. Marriage.
I. Title.
HQ61.P45   301.41   72-4701
ISBN 0-8298-0240-1

CONTENTS

FOREWORD

What does "love" mean? How can we achieve it? What are its hopes and promises? What are the illusions or corruptions which may destroy love?

These questions have constituted a large part of my thinking and teaching for—well, for all my professional life, but more particularly, for the past decade, as I have discussed these questions with college students. In repeated lectures and discussions on many campuses, these efforts at interpretation were shaped and re-shaped.

And what a decade it has been! I can't begin to summarize the "revolutions" which occurred during the sixties. And every new explosion required a new look at what love meant in this new situation. What was new and what might be a replay of an old error? What was change and what might be decadence? What was helpful and what might be damaging? There were no easy answers, but fundamental human values were at stake—and we all knew it.

Then during the past four years the pace of change seemed to quicken, the challenges to conventional values intensified. At the same time, new insights and understandings emerged. So this manuscript has been in the making for four years. It may need four years more. But at some point, I have to be willing—if able —to put some things down on paper. Then they can be evaluated, tested, and hopefully they will prove useful.

In any case, here is one man's attempt to share what he has learned about love. He has learned it from his wife and children, from the Bible, from wise teachers, from friends in and out of the church. He ventures to put it down here in the hopes that what he has learned may be useful to others who want to love and be loved.

He even hopes you're as lucky as he is.

LIBERATED LOVE

1

HOW DOES LOVE HAPPEN?

Love is the nicest four-letter word. Anybody can use it, and almost everybody does. The trouble is we use it so often and so widely that it's hard to know just what the word means.

If we want to experience love ... but the "if" is hardly necessary ... we *do* want to experience love. Therefore, we should take the time to sort out its meanings and decide what it is we want. Then we can ask how it happens.

ONE LITTLE WORD

There is a delightful paragraph somewhere in *Ulysses*, in which James Joyce pokes fun at the various meanings of the word. At least I think that's what he's doing. In any case, it is a humorous and good-natured passage. It may also be a serious indicator of our confusion.

> Love loves to love love. Nurse loves the new chemist. Constable 14A loves Mary Kelly. Gerty MacDowell loves the boy that has the bicycle. M.B. loves the fair gentleman. Li Chi Han lovey up kissy Cha Pa Chow. Jumbo, the elephant, loves Alice, the elephant. Old Mr. Verschoyle with the ear trumpet loves old Mrs. Verschoyle with the turned in eye. The man with the brown macintosh loves a lady who is dead. His Majesty, the King loves Her Majesty the Queen. Mrs. Norman V. Tupper loves officer Taylor. You love a certain person. And this person loves that other person because everybody loves somebody, but God loves everybody.[1]

The fun in the paragraph is obvious. Just as clear to me is a rather deep confusion, which is characteristic of our common talk about love. The same word is used to identify several different kinds of experiences, quite unlike each other, some actually contrary to others. There is childish love, animal love, the love between elderly husband and wife, youthful love, possibly illicit love, and even divine love. One little word is used to designate a striking variety of experiences and relationships. How can we help but be confused as to what it really means?

There seem to be three popular understandings—misunderstandings?—of the word love.

The first is sentimental. Love means to feel nice toward other people, to be always gentle and harmless. The once-popular vogue of "flower power" was surely sentimental.

The classic news photo of the flower being held up to the muzzle of a threatening rifle is an illustration of this. It looks as if the flower might be more powerful than the rifle. But everything depends on what never shows in the picture. Who's at the other end of the rifle? And under what system of controls and rules do both the flower-holder and the rifle-wielder operate? The history of violence in our society—not least on our campuses—illustrates this.

Flower power itself, as a term, may fall out of usage, but the sentiment persists. Just the other day, my wife was given a flower by a "flower person." It was a gentle and kind act. We were sincerely touched. So we say, love conquers all. As if being harmless— "meek," maybe?—is a winner. (Do we really believe it?)

A second understanding of love is biological. In this view, love is a glandular function demanding expression, a pressure to be relieved, an appetite to be satisfied. Love is a biological act to be performed. "To make love" means to engage in certain physiological exercises. This use of the word is so widespread and so obvious as to need no further comment.

A third common interpretation of love is romantic. Love is a warm, exciting feeling you have toward someone else, an attraction toward him or her. Love is something you "fall in" . . . like a ditch! You are going along, minding your own business, and suddenly you fall in love with somebody.

Of course, the fact is that we are being encouraged all the time to expect something like this to happen. Popular songs, movies, and commercial appeals portray this kind of experience as the fun thing. We look for it, hope for it, expect it. It is rather surprising, really, with all the honesty and reality being expressed in current songs and stories, that this romantic notion still persists. But it does—and it sells.

When the romantic is coupled with the biological, we have a combination that is very explosive. John and Mary meet casually . . . there is a magic attraction between them . . . a relationship develops, quite tender and touching . . . nothing permanent, mind you, but nice while it lasts . . . it seems only natural that they go to bed. So we dream that someday the "right" person, or at least a right person will come along, and we'll make the big scene.

But the confusion is not due simply to the pressures of pop culture. There seem to be quite proper variations in the use of the term love. There is the love for some very special person, indeed it may be the one with whom you decide to spend the rest of your life. There is the love between parent and child—both ways. We speak of love for friends and neighbors, our fellowmen. Ideally this extends not only to proper love of country but to a love for humanity. And whether we are concerned personally or not, we know that religious people talk about love in relation to God.

Really, this is an enormous freight for one four-letter

word to carry. When you think of the giggling and groping associated with some uses of the term, and the ecstasy and high-minded service related to other uses, you might wonder whether one word can do it all. Most of us know that the Greeks had three or four words to express these various meanings. We may have to refer to them some time, just for the sake of clarity. But we're committed to one word. And maybe we should see whether there is any common meaning in all the variety of uses.

THE MEANING OF LOVE

Who can help us discover whether there is such a deep and basic meaning to love?

You may reply, "Why make such a big thing of it? Why not just relax and enjoy whatever comes along?"

The answer is that love is too important an experience to be left to chance or to popular pressures. The huckster is out to sell us. He isn't worried about the authenticity of his product, and we don't really expect him to be. Hollywood and the pop music industry are out to entertain us, at their profit. This is fun; we enjoy it. But we don't look to such an enterprise for dependable guidance concerning one of the most significant experiences in our lives. And the purveyors of playboy "philosophy"—male and female alike—hardly offer the depth of judgment and understanding which we need in things that really matter.

It's important that we get our meanings straight in order that our experience may turn out well. If our meanings are confused, we may have a bad trip. Our experiences may prove disappointing or disastrous. Meanings shape our expectations. And if we are hoping for something that is unreal or even dangerous, we will be either disillusioned or damaged.

———◆—◆◆◆—◆———

The importance of clear and accurate definition may be illustrated with respect to another word which is very important today: liberation. Freedom, of course, has always been a great word, and a great human ideal. Men and women committed to liberty, for themselves and others, have helped shape a society which allows us all a considerable measure of freedom. We owe a lot to such people—past and present.

Again today there is much earnest championing of liberation. We can certainly be glad for this. But some of us want to keep raising the question, "What do you mean by liberation?"

A frequent response to such a question is an impatient scepticism. The young and the minorities think we are putting them off—or putting them on. They suspect (and they may sometimes be right) that we are trying to avoid their demand to be allowed to do their own thing.

But that's exactly the point. . . . What *is* your own thing? How can you do your own thing until you know who you really are?

All too often, liberation is taken to mean the freedom to do as you please. And some of us want to call attention to the evidence that that's a good way to destroy yourself. If you reply that you have the right to destroy yourself, if you choose, we have to admit that you do indeed. But you can hardly expect us to applaud such action as either wise or desirable.

Some demands for liberation seem actually to be protests against all restraints or responsibilities. Freedom, it is said, must be "absolute" or it is not real. Some of us want to say that it is precisely "absolute freedom" that is fictional. There is no such thing in human experience. To be human is to live in relationship to other humans. My freedom is always related to someone else's freedom. And mine stops where it damages his, and vice versa.

We humans must always live under some kind of constraints and accept certain responsibilities. If we don't choose our own, some will be forced on us. So freedom may mean the opportunity to choose your own responsibilities, to accept the constraints under which you will live.

Another common confusion is to regard liberation as the rejection of any standard of excellence or value. All actions are regarded as of equal value, and we should be free to do anything that pleases us. But as Norman Cousins points out with his usual incisiveness, this is to confuse "liberation and exhibition."[2] Pleas for liberation may become exercises in exhibitionism. (This reminds me of a comment that was current perhaps a quarter century ago: Some have sought to be liberated, and have succeeded only in becoming unbuttoned!) Cousins' insight is entirely accurate. So is his judgment when he adds, "Liberation is too important to be left to liberators who don't know what liberation is all about, who have little sense of history and even less sense of a vista for the human future."[3]

If you really want to be liberated, you have to discover who you are, who you are intended to be, and who you want to become. These discoveries, which become decisions, have to be made before you can exercise genuine freedom. If what you take to be liberty spoils your integrity, you have not only failed to achieve liberation, you have destroyed a significant freedom.

For instance, liberation is sometimes symbolized by facility in the use of assorted four-letter words. But what will it profit you to be free to shout all the obscenities in the vocabulary, and lose the capacity to appreciate the beauty of language? Some of us want to suggest that you are making a bad trade. What you are losing (which can only be won by discipline) is far more valuable than what you are gaining (which may be only the expression of your own problem with authority).

What if you gain the liberty to play games with your sex, and lose the capacity to enter into sexual activities as a sacramental union? Some of us want to say that this is a poor deal. You are trading off a profound human fulfillment (entered into only by way of commitment) for an intense but temporary excitement (which may be a frustrated attempt to meet an aching inner need which is never satisfied in this way).

Liberation may mean much more than we realize. Its achievement may be at once more difficult and more rewarding than we can guess. Freedom probably means the liberty to become who you are meant to be. This involves courage to be freed from social coercions and wisdom to be released from inner compulsions. Such liberation requires a considerable measure of self-knowledge and self-direction.

By the same token, liberation to love must involve some adequate understanding of what love means. And as we return to this question, we must ask where we can turn for some dependable guidance in seeking the answer.

———————◆◉◆———————

You may think it strange if I suggest that we turn to the psychotherapists, but there are two reasons for this. First of all, they are likely to be men of deep insight and understanding. Their field of study is precisely human beings like ourselves. Secondly, their intent is to help us live better. They may be making a living at it, but that's no disgrace. Their living is helping people.

If you are willing to try this, you are probably in for a surprise. Because these therapists, with all their differences, are likely to define love not primarily in terms of feeling or emotion, but in terms of attitude and will. Love is basically your attitude toward other people, your way of relating to them, your willingness to act in certain ways with them.

About a dozen years ago, Erich Fromm wrote a wise little book entitled *The Art of Loving*. In it he defines love as "the active concern for the life and the growth of that which we love."[4] He adds that love is not so much a receiving as a giving. Love is the capacity to give oneself to another person, for the sake of that person himself.

More recently Rollo May has written what I suspect is a definitive treatment of the subject. He titles it *Love and Will*. It is a profound and complex book—as profound and complex as love itself. May contends that our human task is "to unite love and will."[5] One aspect of this is really to care about others, to acknowledge that others really do matter, as much as and perhaps even more than oneself.[6]

Concern. Care. These words indicate the fundamental meaning of love. Goodwill—literally, willing the good of another.

This hardly sounds like what all the fuss is about. Is this what moves the songwriters' pens? What artists and poets and novelists agonize over? Surely, something has been left out of the "definition." It has indeed.

There is another aspect of love. Love also means a profound urge for union with another person.[7] Every one of us is lonely, incomplete. We feel a deep longing for wholeness, a wholeness which we sense can only be experienced in union with someone else. And this seems to be where all the wonderful and bewildering emotions come into play. The agony and the ecstasy of love . . . the sweet mystery and sorrow . . . the hoped-for fulfillment . . . these aspects of love seem to be related to the profoundly personal need to unite with another, to give yourself to another and know that person is similarly given to you.

What becomes clear, then, is that the experience of love looks in two—or is it several?—directions. It is a deeply personal, even intimate experience. It is a longing for personal union with another that surely must be an exclusive experience. You don't go around achieving authentic union with very many people. But love is also the will to seek the good of the other, not only the intimate other, but the human other—friend, neighbor, fellow citizens, some of them deprived and different, all of them members of the human race—anonymous, distant, but human.

HINDRANCES AND HANGUPS

When we think of love in such terms as these, it becomes clear why serious thinkers acknowledge that love is a rare and even difficult achievement. This kind of love doesn't happen as easily as popular songs and stories seem to suggest. And the sad fact is that most of us settle for less, maybe even for false forms of love that can't possibly yield the satisfaction we want.

That may be too placid a way to put it. There is evidence that living without love is a desperate kind of agony, and that many people know it. One of Dostoevski's characters cries out, "What is hell? I maintain that it is the suffering of being unable to love." Apparently, plenty of people are living in such a hell.

Some of you may ask, "What do you mean being unable to love? Who can't love? Surely, this is something anybody can do? Are you saying that love is an ability to be gained somehow?" Such a suggestion runs contrary to most of our popular expectations. But it may be worth taking seriously.

I can still remember an occasion when I was talking

with some students and said something about learning to love. The students looked at me with shocked unbelief. As if love had to be learned! Anybody knows that love comes naturally, they said.

I could only reply by asking where they were learning what love means. Who were their teachers about love? And, sure enough, it was pop music, movies, and playboy journalists. Add a few gurus, mostly theoretical and sentimental, and you have the "primary sources" for current notions of love.

All I can say is that if you want to experience human love as it really can be, you must graduate from this level of learning and move on to something more authentic. You must choose between being profound or frustrated.

It is not easy to love, really to love. And the first thing we have to learn is why. Here we are in for another surprise. Because the toughest hindrances are right inside ourselves. If we are to love, we have to understand and, hopefully, ease the hangups which prevent us from loving. Let me mention just two.

The first is fear. It's difficult to love because we are afraid. Aldous Huxley has written somewhere that if love casts out fear, it is also true that fear casts out love. He is exactly right.

Recently I was talking with a psychiatrist. He said to me, "I think young people are scared."

I looked at him in surprise. This was hardly my impression of today's youth. So I asked, "What do you mean?"

He replied, "They're really afraid to give themselves to what genuine love requires of them."

I think I know what he means. Loving someone, in the sense of giving yourself, really puts you in an exposed position. To love someone is to expose your "real self." And the minute you do that, you can get hurt.

Your real self may not be all that attractive. So you put up a good front. After all, other people may not like the real you. So put up a front that you think they will like. Even with that special person or those few special people whom you want to love you, the tendency is to show them what they'll like.

Besides, how do you know you can trust them? If you really open yourself to them, they can take advantage of you. That's a good way to get hurt. So keep your guard up: Don't let anybody get too close, until you can be real sure.

Talk about being uptight! Yet, with all our talk about openness and honesty, this is the way most of us feel we have to be. And love doesn't happen that way.

A second hangup is simply our natural self-centeredness. After all, every one of us is born with a central interest in his own well-being. To ask me to act out of honest concern for your well-being is to ask a great deal. Moreover, with my natural suspicion of your own self-interest, I'm not too ready to believe that you are eager to act out of concern for me. So we spar with each other, feinting and ducking; not giving any more than we have to, and not expecting to get anything extra either; careful that somebody else won't take advantage of us, but willing to use advantage for our own interest when we get the chance. And love doesn't happen—often not even in our most personal relationships.

In a current "novel" there's a brief little scene between a mother and a son. The exchange is a meaningless command from her and a meaningless reply from him. The comment is "When she left, it was as if she had never been there at all."[8]

This reminded me sharply of a scene in a movie which I probably will never forget. It was *The Misfits,* an important movie in its day. Marilyn Monroe is in Reno for a divorce. She is rehearsing the lines which she must repeat before the officer who will grant the divorce. Suddenly she bursts out in anguish, "Why can't I say he wasn't there. I mean, you could touch him, but he wasn't there."

Her friend replies, "If that were sufficient cause for divorce, there wouldn't be a dozen marriages left in the country." Nobody in the audience laughed—or only nervously.

And a line by a contemporary poet haunts me. He muses about a man and his wife: "In one bed and apart."

Maybe this suggests another way to describe love: the capacity to be there for another person. If we are to accomplish this, it looks as if we have to be freed up from these—and who knows how many other?—hangups. We have to move from fear to trust, from self-centeredness to caring about others. But how?

HOW DOES IT HAPPEN?

As I understand Fromm and May, they are saying basically the same thing in somewhat different ways. If you and I are to become able to love, we must be given a love—free and undeserved—which will release us from our hangups, and enable us to give ourselves in the acts and arts of love. But it looks as if no one can love us in this way, unless we are lovable enough to win such love.

Love evokes love. If I am to love, someone must love me. But as long as I am unloving, who will love me?

Ideally, this is supposed to happen to us in the family. Parental love is intended to be a freely-given love. I don't love my children because they deserve it. They frequently don't, and they know it as well as I do. But I love them . . . just because they're my children. At least, that's the way it's supposed to work.

But it wasn't quite that smooth for most of us. And we don't manage to make it quite that smooth for our children. As a matter of fact, if two recently popular movies are at all accurate reflections of what happens in American families, we're in a bad way. If *The Graduate* represents a not untypical gentile family, and if *Goodbye, Columbus* is representative of a Jewish family, the Hebrew-Christian tradition has had it! Whatever the younger generation is doing in these families, there certainly isn't any significant relationship of love between parents and children. The parents don't care for their children as real persons.

Yet, if I understand the therapists as they study our human situation, they are saying that we need to be

27

given a love which will evoke our own capacity to love. Someone—family, friend, lover—must be willing to give himself or herself to you sufficiently to free you from your distrust, sufficiently to win your trustful self-giving. Someone must care enough for you to will your good, and thus evoke your concern for him and others.

In *Soul on Ice,* Eldridge Cleaver gives a touching account of a man who came to teach prisoners at Folsom Prison, where Cleaver was. This man was so sensitive, so intense, that Cleaver took to calling him "the Christ."

One week "the Christ" lectured on love, and assigned the men to write an essay on the subject. Cleaver wrote that he could not love white people, and quoted a sentence from Malcolm X: "How can I love the men who raped my mother, killed my father . . ."

"The Christ" could not accept such a statement, and Cleaver could not change it. The paper was returned, ungraded, spotted by the teacher's tears.

"Jesus wept," comments Cleaver—and is more deeply moved than he realizes by this man's love.[9]

Love doesn't just happen. It must be willed to happen.

———————— ◆•◆•◆ ————————

Now let me bring in those Greek words. I'd like to refer to the way in which Rollo May uses them, in a most dramatic summary of our human condition.

The words and their definitions are these. *Eros* means love as the profound, creative urge in us, which in personal relations is the longing to establish union with another. *Philia* means brotherly love, concern for our fellow humans. *Agape* means an unselfish love which is undeserved but freely given.

Here is May's summary of our need for love.

> Sex is saved from self-destruction by eros.
>
> But eros cannot live without philia.
>
> Philia, in turn, needs agape. [10]

And do you happen to know where that word agape came from? It was injected into our Western vocabulary by a man named Paul. Before he used it, it was quite obscure. But it was the only Greek word which he could find to indicate the love of God which is manifest in Jesus Christ.

You can make of this what you will. But it suggests something which is worth more than casual attention.

There just happens to be a profound and persistent tradition in our culture which affirms that you are loved. Eternally and unchangingly, you are loved. No matter who you are or what happens to you, you are loved.

You'd better believe it.

2

LOVE AMONG THE RUINS

We can't talk about love very long without raising the subject of sex. In fact, there's not much hesitancy about raising the subject nowadays. We are eager to discuss sex. We are anxious to understand it and relate it to the rest of our lives.

How else can we explain the fact that recently three books on the best seller nonfiction list dealt with sex? At least two of them were serious inquiries into a complex subject. (The other could have been challenged at this point.) And it is worth noting that they were not aimed at the young but at adults. Clearly, adults are as interested and anxious and uncertain as youth appear to be.

Our curiosity is matched only by our confusion. We are as unsure about sex as we are about love. There is no public consensus concerning what values should be championed and which ones discarded. In fact, we are not even sure what values are at stake. So once again we have to inquire into a meaning. What is the significance of our sexuality?

WHAT'S NEW?

First of all, however, I think we ought to take a hard look at the uncertainty—I have said confusion—which characterizes our thinking and talking about sex. Why are we so mixed-up, or at least so unsure of ourselves?

It is a cliché to say that we are living in a period of cultural crisis. But like many clichés, the statement is also true. Our crisis is frequently called a revolution. In fact, we seem to be having a whole series of revolutions. And among them is what is sometimes called the sexual revolution.

The signs of the sexual revolution are clear enough. Sex has become what *Time* recently called "a spectator sport."[1] The extent of nudity on stage and screen could hardly have been imagined a few years ago. And the addiction to profanity in language brings barracks-room words into the parlor, boys'-dorm words into the student union.

Some people ask whether there is anything different about this present crisis. After all, there's nothing new about erratic sexual behavior. It seems to be one of humanity's favorite sports. And there have been cultural crises before. What's so special about this one?

Personally, I think there are several new factors in our current collage of revolutions. For one thing, there is a new openness about all sorts of subjects. Particularly in the realm of sexual behavior, matters are openly discussed today that would hardly have been mentioned publicly just a few years ago.

Contraception, abortion, homosexuality, masturbation, orgasm—all of these subjects are completely out in the open today. Almost any issue of the daily paper carries an article—if not several—about these matters. "The pill" designates one particular kind of pill, the purpose of which is almost universally known, certainly in our country.

Just a few days before writing these paragraphs, there appeared a large ad in our local newspaper, announcing a week-long TV series on the homosexual. The ad—it must have been at least a quarter of the page—featured a picture of two men embracing. Frankly, I question the taste of such a display, along with the copy which suggested that, if you didn't have nerve enough to watch the program, you weren't willing to face reality. But there can be no question about the openness of it all.

A Congressional hearing on the pill gave rise to a spate of articles in the papers that would have been inconceivable a few years ago. The testimony that the pill might have serious side effects stirred up a nearly hysterical reaction. Articles about women stopping the pill, and all the unwanted pregnancies that would result, and descriptions of alternate methods of contraception ... this whole "secret" aspect of one of the most intimate areas of a person's life was spread all over our papers. And how many youth may have wondered whether they were the result of an "unwanted pregnancy"—that is anybody's guess.

I'm not making any moral judgments, just describing the facts as they appear to be. If you ask for an evaluation, I should reply that such openness is basically good, though it may easily become exhibitionism. But it is an illusion to think that this in itself will solve any problems. In any case, openness is here. Anything can be talked about, almost anywhere.

A second changing factor is a new sense of freedom, especially on the part of women. I suppose the pill itself has had a lot to do with this. But it's more than just freedom in relation to sex.

The women's liberation movement has captured the attention of the entire nation. Women are demanding that they be regarded as fully equal to men in just about every respect. And I must confess that I am deeply impressed with much that I read and hear about the subject.

In relation to our particular discussion here, such liberation would include freedom for a woman to seek out and enter into any kind of sexual relationship she desires. The argument is that a woman should have the same opportunity to enjoy sexual experiences as men have traditionally had, with no more moral condemnation than men have conventionally suffered. As one who has long championed a single standard of morality, I find a strong cogency in this argument—even though the single standard I have championed is quite different from permissiveness.

But there is something still deeper in our current revolution. In a way which has never been true before, at least in recent experience, the very standards by which behavior is evaluated are being challenged, even discarded. What were once regarded as desirable values are now being tested and examined.

For instance, there's nothing new about young men and young women engaging in sexual play before marriage. In previous times, however, those who did this had a sneaky sense that they were doing something wrong, or at least that they were breaking accepted standards of behavior.

But now young men and young women are asking, "Who says it's wrong?" The very values that once were regarded as desirable—chastity, virginity, and such—are being questioned. And the reply to the challenge has to be something other than an appeal to tradition or convention.

A Note About Pornography

Let me illustrate what I take to be a really new element in our contemporary crisis by a brief note about pornography. There's nothing new about pornography. Curiously enough, it seems to be universal and persistent in most "advanced" cultures.

What is new is that today we don't seem to know what pornography is. How do you determine what picture or which written description is pornographic? Or should we say obscene? We no longer know how to answer the question. Our courts have tried a definition of obscenity. It is being tested repeatedly, and I would have to say it is being reduced to an almost undefinable term.

As a result, books are published and openly available which, if they aren't pornographic, are hardly distinguishable from the real thing. The cult of nudity in girly (and now boy, and girl-and-boy) magazines goes to new lengths of voyeurism. And most of this has happened in the past few years.

In fact, the pace of change is constantly increasing. Nothing illustrates this fact better than this very page. The preceding paragraphs were first written about six months before this present one. And already the situation has changed.

The issue now is no longer a definition of pornography. The present question is whether what is admittedly hard core pornography should be openly available to "consenting adults." In fact, right now hard core pornography can be seen in regular movie houses.

That's how fast things have moved in six months. And it's hard to guess where they may be headed when this paragraph appears in print. I think the direction is clear. We are headed for more and more open pornography ... or as a sensitive friend prefers to call it, obscenity. The question is how do we respond to this prospect.

What concerns me is not that pornography will make sex criminals of its users. What worries me is that it may spoil our expectations of sex. It may spoil our chance of entering into a really beautiful relationship with someone for whom we care deeply and to whom we would like to give ourselves for real.

I'm not ready to commit myself as to what should be done concerning the regulating of pornographic materials. I repeat my concern, however, which is not that using pornography will make people sex criminals. My fear is that it may spoil our expectations of what sexual experience with someone we care for should and can be.

Moreover, it isn't only hard core pornography that can have this effect, but also the near-pornography that characterizes so much of our fiction and so many of our movies. I can't help but wonder what happens to the imaginations of all the people who read the current sensational novels. Do they dream of having similar acts performed on themselves, or doing such things to others? And do their fantasies become realities? Or do they suffer frustration that their real lives don't yield such fantastic opportunities?

And the effect of all this on our values and expectations really concerns me. Let me cite an eloquent illustration of this from a most perceptive article which appeared in *The New Yorker*. This particular paragraph is entitled simply "Health."

The bus passes a movie house featuring a film notorious for its obscene bluntness. One of two boys about fourteen years old who are sitting across from me asks, "Have you seen it?" "Yes," the second answers. "It's nothing special." And

he shrugs with a convincing lack of involvement.
The boy doesn't know it, but he is already
crippled.[2]

The author is quite right. And that's what scares me
about much of the stuff that is being pushed today,
often in the name of freedom. I have no desire to deny
you the freedom to look at whatever you want to look
at. But I hate to have you spoil something that is really
quite beautiful.

HOW DID WE GET HERE?

In any case, here we are. And now I want to ask a
question which you may not expect. How did we get
here? Your first reaction to such a question may be
negative.

Students have been labeled—and wear the label
rather proudly—the NOW generation. This means that
they are intent on living in the immediate present. They
are not at all certain of their future. One of their most
sympathetic teachers has put it very well: "I think I
know what is bothering the students. I think that what
we are up against is a generation that is by no means
sure that it has a future."[3] Or, as another teacher quotes
them, "The future is now."[4]

By the same token, students are not much interested
in the past. History is a discipline for which they have
little or no sympathy. They're not interested in how we
got here. Here we are ... NOW ... let's get on with it.

At this point, students have an ironic kinship with
their elders. There's little generation gap here. It was
one of the industrial heroes of an earlier generation

38

who said, "History is the bunk." Add a few obscenities, and you can hear the same sentiment on many campuses today.

Strange bedfellows: student radical and pioneer industrialist! And both equally undependable at this point.

Sooner or later we're going to have to admit that this is a very dishonest and unrealistic attitude. NOW didn't happen today, or even yesterday. Today has been a long time getting here. And we really can't understand our moment in time, or even ourselves, without some sense of how we got here. The meaning of love, of sex, the so-called sex revolution . . . these have a history.

After all, the student generation didn't invent sex. They didn't even start the sex revolution. They surely didn't make the standards they are rebelling against. But just as surely they didn't invent the standards they would like to adopt. All these facts have a history.

Let me put it as clearly as I can. The present revolutionary crisis in which we are involved had its origins at least as far back as World War I. That's fifty years ago . . . almost sixty now. We are caught up in the advanced stages of a cultural process—I call it a cultural drift—that began a half century ago.

If we are going to live well in our present, we must have some sense of how we got here and where we may be going. Let me try to document this claim. I would like to offer it as a serious little piece of cultural interpretation. You may test it and take it apart, find it valid or unconvincing. But it makes a lot of sense to me, so I want to set it out here. And I do it under one of my favorite titles . . .

LOVE AMONG THE RUINS

This title belonged to Browning first. He wrote a poem in which a shepherd anticipates meeting his lover among the ruins of a once-splendid city, now overgrown with meadow and returned to pastoral peace. It's all about as remote from our present as anything you could imagine—except perhaps the shepherd's romantic conclusion: "Love is best."

I first met the title, however, as the heading of an article in a *Harper's* magazine in the year 1934. Note the date—1934. The subject of the article is the then NOW generation's concern about love and sex. The author's thesis is that "Browning's 'ruins' were the vestiges of a buried city; our 'ruins' are the vestiges of a buried world."[5]

I was a naive young college student. And I can still remember the shock and dismay with which I read the author's conclusion: "Whatever you may think of it on ethical grounds, the fact remains that the majority of young Americans are living together before marriage."[6]

We understand—with a superior grin—the euphemism of that last phrase. We would hardly need to resort to it today, which is a measure of the change which has occurred. But the claim is clear: The majority of students and young adults were engaging in sexual intercourse before marriage, long before what we call our revolution, long before sociological researches into the curious sexual habits of the American public.

What year was that?

1934 . . . more than thirty-five years ago!

In the years since that shock to my innocence, evidence gathered in my studies and readings indicated that something serious had happened to our American culture. And somewhere in those years I came to suspect that the moment of critical change could be located at World War I. So I began to think and to say that World War I was a cultural shock from which our civilization has never recovered. At that time, something happened to the traditional standards of sexual conduct. Values were challenged and changed. And ever since then, we have been drifting away from conventional certainties into greater permissiveness and deeper confusion.

For years this has been little more than a hunch. It was a hunch that fit in with much that I had learned ... but still a guess. You can imagine, then, that I have been pleased in recent studies to add a little documentation to the claim.

The crucial evidence appears in Kinsey's study of sexual behavior. Let me cite the conclusion as stated in a book written specifically about sex as a concern of the college generation.

> The real change (in sexual morality) came with the generation born between 1900 and 1910, who were in their teens just after World War I. Since then there has been a progressive trend toward justifying sexual freedom, or rather a progressive repudiation of the need to justify one's natural inclination.[7]

Then the author adds a statement which may be a blow to the pride of some, but here it is: "The actual practice of this generation (the present student generation) is very little different from that of those who graduated forty years ago."[8]

Let me relegate the relevant Kinsey quote to a footnote. I don't want to bore you with quotations. But I have enough respect for your intellectual honesty to let you know where the evidence is.[9]

Rollo May voices the same conclusion, in a somewhat less sympathetic manner.

> Then, in the 1920's, a radical change (from Victorian attitudes towards sex) occurred almost overnight.... In an amazingly short period following World War I, we shifted from acting as though sex did not exist at all to being obsessed with it. We now place more emphasis on sex than any society since that of ancient Rome, and some scholars believe we are more preoccupied with sex than any other people in all of history.[10]

Are you willing to accept the possibility that something happened fifty years ago that helped determine where we are now? I'm sorry about what this does to anyone's sense of being the NOW generation. It means that NOW is a half century old! Because I have a second part to this thesis.

———— ◆•◆ ————

From that time to the present, we have been in a period of cultural drift. We have never recovered from the blow to conventional cultural standards and practices. What was started then was irreversible. We have drifted. There has been no effective influence to slow down or alter the direction of cultural change. There has been a lot of talk, a lot of protest, as well as a lot of cheering. But the process has been all in one direction —toward greater permissiveness, toward the elimination of conventional practices and standards.

Let me be clear that I'm not making moral judgments —not at the moment, anyway. I'm trying to identify and describe a cultural event and its subsequent developments. I'm trying to tell it like I think it is. Maybe it would help if I illustrated this process of drift.

Try to put yourself in the place of some of those previous generations. How far back should we go? Back to me?

It was 1934 when I, as a college student, read that maybe half my contemporaries were going to bed together. That was, let's say, fifteen or twenty years after World War I. We were already the children of the first generation to feel the cultural shock. Was our behavior the result of what they had or hadn't taught us? The subtle example our parents had or hadn't given us?

Anyhow, let's admit that a good many of our generation were playing around in the 30's. Then we got married. What did we tell our children about sex? What could we tell them? We probably tried to do the conventional thing, and say that it was naughty. But we had been playing around before—maybe we still were—and our teaching couldn't have been very convincing. And what kind of examples could we offer?

Then came World War II. This was another moral shock, compounding the cultural crisis set off by World War I.

In the meantime, with standards and practices loosening up, youth continued to get married and raise families. What did these parents, who themselves had been increasingly permissive in their behavior, tell their children?

There's one other factor I have to put in here, even if it betrays my bias. All the time that these standards were loosening and behavior was changing, the traditional basis for these values was being neglected—and perhaps even undermined. Moral standards do not stand alone. They are always part of a cultural and religious complex. And during the fifty-year period I am talking about, the total cultural and religious context of conventional morality was undergoing serious change. (I almost said "deterioration," but that's a loaded word. Let it stand as "change.")

This observation is important. I can't develop it extensively here, but let me illustrate it from a recent movie review.

The movie is *The Passion of Anna,* hailed by many as Bergman's greatest film. It is a very glum portrayal of a dull kind of life. Why? One character is an architect who comments that his works are merely "mausoleums over the meaninglessness in which most of us live." I claim that this meaninglessness is what cuts the ground from under our ethical values and leaves us without standards of value and judgment. Interestingly enough, a critic of the film supports my contention in a very telling comment.

"I am not religious," she writes, "but I can see how much our atheist epoch may have impoverished Western art by formulating no substitute order of good and evil." And not just art, I would say, but life itself. Because, as she continues, in the whole realm of ethical decision "one simply misses somewhere to put one's feet, it seems that there is no floor—only falling."[11]

"No floor—only falling." Exactly. And what do you stand for, when there is no dependable footing? The answer is we are fair game to fall for anything.

So now here we are. After several generations of drifting, traditional standards themselves are being challenged at a level deeper than ever before, with a seriousness seldom experienced in the history of our civilization.

NOW is over thirty! Today has been fifty years getting here. Youth didn't make it. They inherited it.

Students seem aware of this in terms of other cultural problems, such as war and race. They know they didn't make today's world. Their parents did. And our children are pretty well fed up with the mess we've made.

What I'd like to say to students and young adults is something like this: Why should you think you've been any more original in the matter of sex practices? Is it possible that you've inherited a mess at this point, as you have at so many others. In any case, admit that you haven't originated much yet. Most of it is fifty years old.

Now I know very well that a cultural shock such as World War I doesn't just blast off all of a sudden. The crisis of the twentieth century is rooted in a still deeper crisis . . . let me say it, a crisis of faith . . . which pervades our whole civilization. I should like to discuss this more thoroughly, but it would take us too far afield.

I think there is need for a careful look at our recent cultural history. (Another time, maybe!)

For now, I want to persuade you to consider the possibility that the NOW in which we are living is a half century old. There are distinctive and intense marks of our own special time. But much of what we are struggling with has been shared by others. (Chastity was a problem for my generation—believe it or not.) And where we are today can best be handled, if we remember how we got here.

What's so important about all this?

Well, among other things it means that you can't assume that what is NOW is good. You can't simply take it for granted that the developments of the past half century represent progress. It is naive to accept current ideas about the meaning of love and sex. If it is true that we've been drifting with a cultural current for a half century, then contemporary pop culture is not all that original. It may be confused—even corrupt. It is entirely possible that in this profoundly important area of life, we are being sold a bill of goods. You may buy it, thinking that you're being terribly original and emancipated. But you may be buying an old error dressed up in mod styles.

This is my plea to the NOW generation . . .

Don't be naive.

It doesn't surprise you when today's merchants try to sell you an article that is shoddy or cheap, just so they can make a buck. You've learned to expect this—

and to sneer at it. Do you imagine that the appropriate merchants would be any less hesitant to sell you shoddy ideas about sex and love?

Don't be naive.

You are properly irritated that the generations before you have carelessly polluted the atmosphere and water until we are at a really dangerous point in the way we treat our environment. Do you think for a moment that these same generations would be any more careful in their pollution of your ideas and practices, even if they endangered your life?

Don't be naive.

Do you imagine that a generation that would peddle cancer-inducing habits would hesitate to peddle values and ideals that might eat away your integrity?

Don't be naive.

What you have to do is stop and ask . . . Where are we? . . . How did we get here? . . . Whom can I trust?

My fear is that youth will be taken in before they have a chance to think clearly for themselves. In fact, this is what happens. Pop culture has already shaped our values and our habits, even before we have had a chance to think about them. Then when we are already stuck with them, we justify them by the same pop merchants who sold us in the first place!

And we call it NOW. Revolution!

My plea is . . . don't be naive. Let's look at these matters much more carefully than our peers, or the merchants who are selling us and our peers, are ever likely to encourage us to do.

Then if you want to buy what seems to be the current

crop of liberated ideas, you're welcome to them. But don't call it "revolution." You're just buying into a NOW that is fifty years old. You'd better look it over first.

Fortunately, among the ruins there are also resources. We know a lot more today, about all sorts of things, than we ever did before. This includes love and sex. And here again I turn to the scientists who are most deeply engaged in the study of man. There is not unanimity among them, of course. But there is a fund of wisdom. And we would be wise to draw upon it.

3

LOVE AND SEX: BEYOND MORALITY

Love and sex go together like love and marriage. At least, that's what some of us used to think. But divorce is playing havoc with both connections. We all know that there are marriages without love or that love can go out of a marriage. Similarly, some are now saying that sex need have no particular connection with love. It may, they say, but it need not.

Carnal Knowledge is a sensitive movie that dramatizes such a separation. Sexual acts between the characters are just what the title says: carnal knowledge, body sensations without any deeper significance. Where "love" seems, for a while at least, to be involved, it is an immature attraction. And sex without love turns out

49

to be a joyless business—perhaps ultimately "un-sexing." The movie seems to say, "Enough of this car-nal knowledge and you'll destroy yourself."

So we had better take a long look at the question we stirred up earlier. What is the meaning of sex? Just as we have tried to define rather carefully what the word "love" means, we must give equal care to our under-standing of the word "sex."

THE MEANING OF SEXUALITY

What is the significance of sex? What does it mean to be male or female?

We talk a lot, and think a lot, about our humanity. What does it mean to be human? Not very long ago, it dawned on me that we are never simply human. Every one of us is either male human or female human.

You'd think after several decades of being one of these, I'd realize it might be important. But it was only a comparatively few years ago that it really got through to me that I am not just human . . . I am male human. My humanity is inseparable from my maleness. My wife's humanity is inseparable from her femaleness. When I ask what it means to be a human creature, I must ask also what it means to be a sexual creature.

Here we run into a fundamental difference of inter-pretation. And I suppose you have to take your choice. Let me try to state what the alternatives are, and in the process my own judgment will become clear enough.

The pop view of sex is that sex is a biological urge, the release of which is accompanied by intensely pleasurable feelings. The standard for sex behavior, then, is to gain and give whatever pleasure you can, as long as nobody gets hurt.

The fundamental meaning of sexuality, in this view, is biological and hedonistic. Sex is a pleasure-producing, biological act. The possible consequences, in terms of conceiving a child, are incidental to the continuation of the race, and do have certain social implications. But these consequences do not define the meaning of sex. Sex is recreational. It is for fun.

Albert Ellis is a champion of this view. He is a psychologist and a prolific writer. He must be taken seriously. His position is basically what I have just stated. Let me cite a sentence which seems to summarize his belief:

> Every human being, just because he exists, should have the right to as much (or as little), as varied (or as monotonous), as intense (or as mild), as enduring (or as brief) sex enjoyments as he prefers—as long as, in the process of acquiring these preferred satisfactions, he does not needlessly, forcefully, or unfairly interfere with the sexual (or non-sexual) rights and satisfactions of others.[1]

Or, more simply stated, "everyone has a human right to sex-love involvement of his own taste, preference, and inclination."[2]

That seems simple enough—and the author makes it unmistakably clear in his other essays. Anything goes, as long as it is mutually desirable and not hurtful to either participant. Sex in any style or circumstance is permissible: with or without love, hetero- or homo-, premarital, marital, or extramarital. Sex is for fun.

Underlying this standard of value is the interpretation of sex as a simple biological release. This becomes apparent in the various figures of speech which Ellis uses to illustrate his points. The risk of secret adultery, without the knowledge of your mate, is comparable to buying a Cadillac or accepting a new job without telling the other. Preference for one style of sex over another is comparable to preferring classical to popular music, or Hamlet to quiz shows. You might prefer steak to candy, but why try to prohibit people from eating sweets? And who would think of eating nothing but meat and potatoes?[3]

Well, that's all logical enough. If sex is a biological appetite with pleasurable effects, enjoy it. However, we should not overlook the warning voiced by one wise observer, a highly trained scientist: "When sex becomes a sport or fun and nothing else, it generally ceases to be fun."[4]

But what if our sexuality means something in addition to biology . . . maybe even something more than biology? This possibility has to be considered, because it is exactly what other profound thinkers are telling us.

———————◆●� ●◆———————

Our sexuality is one of the deepest aspects of our humanity. It is profoundly linked to some of the basic drives of our being . . . deeper than mere biology . . . right in the very core of our being. This is seen in a couple of ways.

Sexuality is the expression of our profound longing for wholeness. Human wholeness is neither male nor female but male-with-female. To be male means to need —profoundly to need—union with the female. To be female means to long for—deeply to long for—union with the male. Our humanity can be complete only with the union of male and female. And our sexuality is at once the sign and means of this union.

This is one aspect of the meaning of sex which men like May and Fromm try to communicate.[5] And interestingly enough, they document this not only out of their own medical practice, but also out of the wisdom of the race as expressed in ancient myths.

There is a Greek myth which portrays the original human creature as possessing both sexes in one being. Somehow, this creature was split apart. And ever since, the two halves—male and female—long to regain their original unity. Eldridge Cleaver refers to this cleavage as the "Primeval Mitosis." He sees humans as being driven by an irrepressible longing for "Apocalyptic Fusion."[6] The language and the figures of speech may vary, but the intention is clear. There are important indications that our sexuality is deeper than biology. It is rooted in our very being, as a longing for wholeness, the union of male and female.

The other aspect of the meaning of sex is the profound relation of our sexuality to our fundamental human creativity. Thus May links sex to eros, which he defines as our longing for beauty and achievement, our urge to create. He affirms that sex becomes destructive when it is separated from eros, and the essential link between the two must be restored.[7]

The sign of this relation between sexuality and creativity is that sex is procreative. With all our current cleverness about contraception, we are likely to lose sight of this fundamental fact. One intention of sex is, after all, the conception and procreation of children. And in thinking about the meaning of sex, this simple fact must be acknowledged. Its significance is more than just biological. It's not just a trick that nature has played on us to ensure the continuation of the race. It is an aspect of our fundamental human need for union and for creativity.

———————◆•◦•◆———————

These two considerations, taken together, suggest the reasons why some of us are convinced that sex is more than fun and games.

First of all, sex is not just an energy to be released, a pressure to be relieved, an appetite to be satisfied. It may indeed be these. But it is also much more. Therefore, figures of speech which reflect this view, and which are so frequent in popular discussion of the subject, are woefully inadequate and deceptive. The need for sex simply is not comparable to our need for food.

Our sexuality is also a profound longing for wholeness, for union with a human counterpart. We long, irrepressively and at the deepest part of our being, for a complete and fulfilled humanity. Sexual union is the symbol and expression of that longing. The sex act is the connection which makes possible our wholeness.

Secondly, the meaning of sex is also—and unavoidably—procreational. The intent of sex is not only recreational but also procreational. And no amount of contraceptive cleverness can ever erase this meaning. We can avoid the issue, yes, but not the intent.

This doesn't mean that we have to be willing to conceive a child every time we have intercourse. But it means that when we embrace the act, we must be willing also to embrace its meaning. The connection between the sex act and its intended issue is too profound to be casual. Our sexuality carries with it this meaning. And we must be willing to enter into its total significance.

Geneticists and other scientists in the field of human reproduction assure us that the time will come when sexual intercourse will be "totally severed" from the conception and birth of children. They say we will reproduce children quite without sexual intercourse. Therefore, our sexuality may seem to have little or no relation to procreation.

I would maintain that even when this time comes, the meaning of sexuality cannot be separated from its built-in intention. We are talking here not about technology but about teleology, not just practice but also purpose. And at this point, I stand with the insights of the psychotherapist as well as with the interpretations of the technologist.

It is true that the manipulation of sex can be separated from its procreative possibilities. But the meaning of sex can never be separated from its procreative purpose. You can have the thrill of sex and avoid conception. But to experience the fulfillment of sexuality, you must be willing to affirm your creativity.

Sex is fun. Of course, it is. And nobody knows it

better than two well-married people. But having said this, we've said hardly anything. Because sex is infinitely more than just fun. It is the sign and sacrament of union, the means and mystery of creativity. This is why some of us believe that sex is not for kicks but for keeps.

—————————◆•◆—————————

Let me try to say this rather directly, and in doing so, to indicate another misunderstanding from which I think we suffer today. Making love is more than just having—or giving—an orgasm. One author has suggested that nowadays we are suffering under "the tyranny of the orgasm." He is quite right.

One evidence is our intense concern with the orgasmic experience. We are solemnly intent on the methodology of getting and giving orgasms. Books are written, illustrated manuals are made available . . . and now, movies are enacting all the details.

Technique is certainly important. It would be foolish to spoil our relationships just because of limited knowledge. But the value or success of the relationship of love certainly should not be measured by the frequency or intensity of orgasmic responses.

We sometimes seem to crave orgasm as if it were the *summum bonum* of existence. Thus, Norman Mailer writes of the "apocalyptic orgasm." He speaks of love as "the search for an orgasm more apocalyptic than the one which preceded it."[8] The compulsive obsession with such an experience must be the most frustrating illusion by which one can be driven. That way lies the destruction of love.

The deeper truth seems to be that we are drawn to the act of sexual congress by a far more profound need than intense pleasure. D. H. Lawrence may not always be the best guide to the understanding of our sexuality. But I believe his insight into its profound significance is certainly looking in the right direction. In one of the scenes in *Lady Chatterley's Lover* the gardener-lover says of his own sex organ, "He's got his roots in my soul!"

The language may be strange or strained—as the whole character may be. But the comment is not without its validity. Any man who has loved deeply knows that the roots of his sexuality are far more profoundly imbedded in his personality than merely in the sex organs which produce spasms of pleasure.

Incidentally, Lady Chatterley is portrayed as knowing this about herself too. It is to Lawrence's credit that he perceived this aspect of our humanity—both male and female—and tried to express it. If his artistic vision occasionally faltered, he was nonetheless seeing far beyond most of his contemporaries.

And Rollo May, somewhere in the work to which we are referring so often, mentions that "making love" is really quite literally just that. The act of sexual congress is the means by which love is not only expressed but deepened. I used to think the phrase "making love" was a semantic mistake. And as commonly used, it is indeed misleading. But May's insight is entirely persuasive. When two people genuinely love one another, the sex act really "makes love," generates affection, deepens commitment.

Any consideration of the meaning of sexuality has to take the measure of such experiences and insights as these.

A Note About Homosexuality

As part of our new openness, there is a lot of discussion about homosexuality. So a note on this subject seems not only appropriate but necessary.

The meaning of sexuality which I have tried to articulate must be the context within which homosexuality is to be understood. Human sexuality finds its fulfillment in the union of male and female, a union which is both sacramental and creative. If that meaning is authentic, then every sexual relationship will be understood and evaluated in relation to that fundamental intention. We do not modify our meaning in order to accommodate variant practices. Rather, we affirm the meaning, and try to understand various experiences in that light. We have done this with alternate heterosexual possibilities. We would do the same with auto-erotic practices. We will want to do the same with respect to homosexuality.

Homosexuals themselves may not always understand or accept this. As I hear some of them, they are asking that homosexual relations be given the same value, the same recognition, as heterosexual relations. I really don't think we can do this—at least, not without seriously modifying the meaning of sexuality as we have interpreted it here. In pleading for acceptance as a person, the homosexual seems often to demand a reinterpretation of sexuality itself. The latter I cannot do without denying my understanding of human reality. The former I can do with all my heart.

I think it is fair to distinguish between understanding homosexuality as a phenomenon, and accepting the homosexual as a person. As a fact of life, homosexuality must be regarded as an interruption of the true meaning of human sexuality. But the homosexual should be accepted as a person and freely given all the social rights and benefits which belong to him. Let me try to interpret this.

First of all, homosexuality should no longer be regarded as a crime. Of course, society must protect itself against the seduction of the young, molesting, or public indecency. And it does this with regard to heterosexual as well as homosexual acts. But beyond this, private sexual conduct—"between consenting adults" has become the phrase—ought not to be regarded as criminal. Laws should be changed—or disregarded, as seems to be simpler with such laws. Practices of harassment and trapping should be eliminated.

Feelings and attitudes change with greater difficulty. But we should try to gain for ourselves, and encourage in others, attitudes of acceptance and understanding.

Having said this, I still find it necessary to say that the deepest meaning of human sexuality looks to the union of male and female. Homosexual acts can never express the total depth and meaning of our sexual being.

And this is not due simply to social custom and mores. It is grounded in the very nature of our maleness and femaleness.

Much discussion of homosexuality tries to diminish this distinction. A recent article in *Time* brought together the comments of several scholars. All the way through, with only occasional exception, the emphasis seemed to be on social custom or personal taste or "secondary sexual characteristics." One sociologist put it crassly enough: "All of a sudden, I found a new penisology—that somehow the shape of the penis and the vagina dictate the shape of human character."[9]

I think he has misread the evidence. What some of us are trying to say is that the shape of human character is precisely what determines the kind of sexual relations that are most deeply fulfilling. And our character is basically heterosexual—not due to accidents of custom or even of physiology—but due to our very humanity.

Still the fact remains that not everybody can experience this male-female wholeness. The reasons for homosexuality are complex, profound, and apparently still quite unclear to many scientists studying in this field. The reality simply is that some people, for reasons still unknown, are drawn to members of their own sex and not—or not so strongly—to members of the opposite sex.

Such persons must find such authentic, responsible realization of their sexuality as they are able. Surely their powers can be expressed in creative and caring ways. They may find deep and abiding friendships which will carry a measure of the affection and commitment which we humans need. Counselors and friends may give guidance and understanding. And together we can form a community of acceptance and support which we all need.

It is all too true that our actual relations with one another may only occasionally achieve their full meaning. (Happily married people have learned this well, and have learned to turn it to best advantage.) But we know what our sexuality is intended to convey: the hope of wholeness in union with one another; a creativity which finds increasing fulfillment. And if we don't always—or even often—make it, our humanity is sustained by the hope and cleansed by the vision; thus our life together is made more beautiful by our modest achievements.

THE MEANING OF MARRIAGE

There is another meaning to be examined. What about this love and marriage bit? Is there really anything to it?

As a parish minister, I am continually impressed with how consistently people want to get married. We all know the risks involved. The limitations and failures of marriage are publicly exposed and examined. One pair of authors bluntly says, "In the United States the state of marriage is a calamity." And they mean not only the number of divorces but also the number of continuing marriages that are "calamitous."[10]

It is certainly true that among many young adults marriage is regarded with considerable scepticism. They see it as a social institution that has failed, just like every other part of the establishment. Some of them are giving up on it altogether and trying other styles of relationship.

Some scholars say that society has undergone such serious changes that old-style marriages just won't work anymore. Some whose marriages have failed blame it on the peculiar stresses and strains of our time in history.

A very wise observer writes, "They do not realize that marriage has always been an impossible enterprise, or at least a perversely difficult one, and that love has never been very durable, to say nothing of eternal."[11] This is surely an accurate estimate. And every realistic person will take it seriously.

But the fact still remains that most young people want to get married. I am convinced that it can't be only biological need or social custom that drives them to it. There has to be a deeper reason than that.

One of our most persistent hopes is that we can achieve a reasonably successful and permanent marriage. This observation is strengthened by a college poll which indicates that "almost all college students intend to get married—and stay married."[12]

We know that it can't be all hearts and flowers, all romance like moon and June. We know there are great risks involved. But we seem also to know that there is a promise and hope of fulfillment in marriage that is not possible in any other relationship. The union to which our sexuality drives us seems to require some sort of a dependable, permanent relationship. Consequently, in trying to understand our sexuality and in trying to find some guidelines for our sexual behavior, I think we have to consider the meaning of marriage.

What kind of a marriage and family do you want to have? If it doesn't matter to you, or if you are considering a different style of marriage, this question will have no meaning. But I believe that most people want a marriage that is characterized by love and fidelity. They would like to have a family in which there is fun and laughter, real personal growth and development, a sense of achievement and fulfillment.

We all know that such an achievement doesn't come easily. John Updike isn't far wrong in *The Couples* when he comments that "every marriage is a hedged bet."[13] But it's a bet worth taking, a hope worth working for. This is what it means to be a human being . . . to hope for a union with another person, in which each finds his fulfillment in the fulfillment of the other, in which each becomes a whole person in relation to the other.

Such a union clearly requires the integrity of both persons. Trust is essential to authentic marriage. And just because our sexuality is so profound in its significance, sexual faithfulness has been considered an important dimension of this fidelity. The sex act is the symbolic expression of our union. It is not too much to say it is the sacrament of marital union. This is why sexual faithfulness is so highly valued—not just because there are old-fashioned mores, as some teachers thoughtlessly say, but because sex is significant.

Now how do we become such trustworthy persons? How do we develop such a dependable fidelity? Certainly, not by merely signing some papers and going through a public ceremony. We become persons of integrity by a lifetime of faithful decisions. We commit ourselves to particular values, and do whatever is required to achieve these values. We don't gain this commitment and this character after marriage. We bring our values and our faithfulness to our marriage.

Our decision, then, about our present behavior may well be based on our hope for the future achievement of a good marriage. What we do now will help us become the kind of persons who are capable of making a good marriage. Or what we do now may unfit us for such a fulfillment. This, at least, has to be considered.

There are some who argue that sexual experiences before marriage will not interfere with the success of your marriage. Some may even argue that it will help you in your marital adjustments.

There are others who affirm that sexual experimentation before marriage may endanger the possibility of your making a good marriage. No one has yet shown me how a person who has had sexual fun with several partners is suddenly able to settle down to just one. Or doesn't it matter to you?

———————◆•◆•◆———————

But, the popular argument goes, we're not talking about promiscuity. We're talking about meaningful relationships, in which we have something great going for us. And sex is the natural expression of the relation that really means a lot to us.

I hear you. And I believe you. I believe you when you say you are not talking about promiscuity. But again I ask you not to be naive.

Who's not talking about promiscuity? Of course, it depends on your use of words. If promiscuity means having sex relations with a lot of different people during the same period of time, maybe you're right. But how many people, seriatim, constitutes promiscuity?

Who's not talking about promiscuity?

In that curious movie imported from Sweden, the girl has had sex with twenty-three men . . . the current one is number twenty-four . . . and he has a child by another girl to whom he is not married. What do you call that? And what chance do these two have for a meaningful relationship?

That's going too far? Well, how far do you mean?

John and Mary meet at a bar. Go to his apartment. Wake up in bed the next morning. Develop a warm, tender relationship during the day. Decide that she should move in. No hint of permanence, mind you. He's had other girls living with him. She's had sex since she was fifteen—or was it sixteen? So they end up in bed again . . . and only then ask each other their names!

Who's not talking about promiscuity?

Hair? The fabulously successful, self-styled "American tribal love rock musical"? What kind of "love" is expressed in this work? One girl complains that she has been "knocked up by an acid head," when it is another fellow she really likes. Variations of sexual behavior are hymned, but there isn't an honest regard for a girl as a person in the whole play.

Who's not talking about promiscuity?

If permissiveness means an unlimited succession of pleasure-giving partners, and marriage need bring no halt to the procession, what do you want to call it?

You may not be talking about promiscuity. But don't be naive.

Not long ago, I was talking with a young man. He and his girl friend had decided that their relationship had developed to the point where they could properly enjoy going to bed together. He wanted to talk it over with me. What did I think?

I respected the thoughtfulness with which both he and his friend had come to this decision. It was surely a mark of the quality of their relationship and their own honesty.

Naturally, there was no thought of marriage. It might come to that. But it might not. There was no commitment.

I asked the young man a question. "How many such meaningful relationships do you allow yourself or your friend? I mean, when it comes time for you to marry, when you decide that you have met the girl you really want to marry, will it make any difference to you how many such relationships she has had? How many men she's gone to bed with? And done with them all the delightful, intimate things she does with you? How many girls you've gone to bed with? And treated to the same private delights? Will this matter? How many do you allow?"

He didn't answer.

Does it matter?

If it doesn't, go to it.

If it does, you have to make a few decisions about the kind of marriage you want, the kind of person you want to be, and the kind of person you hope to marry. You may want to start being that kind of person right now, building fidelity and trustworthiness, self-respect and respect for another, right now.

———◆—◆●◆—◆———

Several kinds of dissent are waiting to be heard. And we really can't leave the present discussion without hearing them.

First there are those who don't expect to get married. They lack either desire or opportunity. Obviously, they will not base their standards of sexual behavior on such considerations as I have suggested here.

However, some of their value judgments will not be too dissimilar. "What kind of person do I want to be? How do I want to treat other people?" If you are unwilling to use or exploit someone else for your own personal enjoyment, you will be very considerate of his or her values. If your self-respect is important to you, you will think carefully about what you do.

It is such decisions that will define behavior. I offer no ready-made rules. The familiar biblical commandment does not apply to this sort of decision unless, of course, married people are involved. But the values of integrity, honesty, self-respect, regard for others—these values are very important indeed.

Let me add one further word. Such single persons are not at all shut out from authentic experiences of love. They may fail to find—or may choose not to seek—the most satisfying style of sexual satisfaction. But they certainly can experience love as honest caring for the good of other persons. They may love and be loved. Some of the most loving services rendered in society are given by single persons. Most of us who have lived for any time will count several such persons among those who have really cared about us. And we believe that many of them have discovered themselves truly loved.

Another kind of dissent is expressed by those who are sceptical, perhaps even disillusioned, about marriage. I have taken a very high view of the marriage relationship. Is it realistic, or hopelessly idealistic?

Let me say that I believe it is an honest interpretation of marriage. I can't pretend that everybody experiences this kind of union and fulfillment. But I know very well that some people do, and find a profound joy that is greater than they ever imagined possible. And I wouldn't be surprised that many a marriage which looks quite ordinary from the outside is marked by quiet satisfactions and achievements that are very rewarding.

Once in a while, I hear of a couple—usually young—who have married and now resent their loss of freedom.

To any well-married person of some experience this is a sad misunderstanding. It is precisely in the binding commitments of marriage that we have found freedom. Moreover, we have found a fulfillment that we suspect just isn't possible in any other relationship.

The trouble is not with the true meaning of marriage. The trouble may be in the way we come to it. Our expectations may be sentimental and unrealistic. Or they may be cynical and sceptical, or secretly selfish. The trouble may be in our unwillingness to work at the relationship, and at our own hangups, in order to grow into the kind of union marriage can become.

There's nothing wrong with marriage. It's a great institution. What's wrong is with us. We can make it beautiful.

PS

Not a word about a commandment? Not a word about morality?

No. We've gone far beyond commands and morality. Morals only have significance as they are rooted in the kind of fundamental meanings we have tried to expound here. Rules are important only as they embody values.

But would you be surprised to know that there is, in fact, a religious view which puts all this into a beautiful and exciting context? Did you know that there is a splendid story of creation that embodies all these meanings? This is what it tries to say:

1. Our humanity is an endowment of God. Whatever we are, we reflect his image.

2. Our sexuality is a good and beautiful mark of this endowment.

3. However, we blew it. We have mishandled what God has given us. So our sexuality has become all mixed up.

4. God would like to restore as much of the original intent of our humanity as possible. This isn't easy by any means—not even divine means. But he is unswervingly faithful in his will to restore us to our intended fulfillment.

5. If we're willing to accept what he offers, in meaning and motivation and promise, we can find a measure of fulfillment in love that will continually surprise us.

If you had never heard of Adam and Eve, would you believe there might be such a story, carrying such a meaning?

4

CIRCLES OF LOVE

There is another dimension to love. Love as caring for others, as willing the good of others, looks outward, beyond yourself and those closely related to you. Up to this point, we have been looking inward, at our own capacity for and experience of love. But if we are to understand love in its fulness, we must also look beyond ourselves, our "loved ones," to the whole human family.

This concern for others is really quite basic, as I'm sure you realize. Fromm goes so far as to say, "The most fundamental kind of love, which underlies all types of love, is *brotherly love*. By this I mean the sense of responsibility, care, respect, knowledge of any other human being, the wish to further his life."[1] You will endorse this heartily. But be prepared to recognize that when you try to take it seriously, you will be plunged into a bewildering assortment of difficult problems.

———— ◆ ●•● ◆ ————

Let me first suggest a figure of speech which has been useful to me. If it doesn't help you, don't bother with it. But I have found it helpful in the rather confusing task of sorting out the various meanings of love, and seeing their relevance to differing relationships.

It is as if we live in concentric circles of love.

At the center of each person's life is himself. You, your ego, you yourself. Here you live deeply and intimately with yourself, and with God or whatever passes for your god. Only you know yourself, and that only partially. One of the things you know is that you need to be an honestly loving person. And when you are your best self, this is what you want to be.

The most intimate circle of love is, of course, the family. It is in your family that you were nurtured, that you became whatever measure of a person you are. Then there is the family into which you move as an adult, your own family. For a while, you withdraw from the earlier intimacy you experienced in the home. But your hope is to move into another family which you yourself will shape. And here the process of love will continue at a deeper, more mature level.

Then there are the various circles in which you move. Classmates and special friends. Teams and social organizations. Maybe a commune. Business associates, neighbors, community organizations. In each of these there is a proper kind of love, a mutuality of concern and common purpose. Still further, you are a citizen of your nation; a genuine love of country is a valid sentiment.

Then there is the widest circle of all, encompassing our planet and all its inhabitants. This is quite impersonal in the sense that we are seldom acquainted with people who live in these distant areas. But we know we all are travelers in what we have learned to call our spaceship, earth. We share common problems. And we may share a common fate. So there is a proper love for all our fellow humans.

Obviously, the qualities of love will vary in these several circles. The depth and intensity of emotion will be greatly different. The family will elicit our deepest feelings. We will love our own children with an intensity which we cannot possibly bring to our love for the children of Africa, India, or China.

But just as clearly, there will be a common element: goodwill, concern, the willingness to seek the good of these others, whether intimately known or impersonally distant. Our responsibility to those closest to us is most immediate and demanding. But our caring for others will reach out just as far as compassionately possible.

The point I want to make now is that in each circle the quality of our caring may be called "love." We love ourselves, our family, our friends, the Vietnamese, the Russians. In each instance, the word love—while we may not always use it easily—is appropriate.

But it is equally clear that in the several circles, the ways in which we will express our "love" will be greatly different. How we behave toward the Russians may be hardly recognizable as love. We may prefer to use a cooler term, such as justice or goodwill. There will be a fervor, an intensity, about our love in the family which is entirely desirable there and quite inappropriate on the campus or in the neighborhood.

Let's look at some of these circles, and see what happens to love in them.

A SCHOOL FOR LOVE

The most intimate circle of love, I have said, is the family. Indeed, the family is intended to be the school of love. It is here that we should learn what love means, as children in relation to our parents and our siblings, and as parents in relation to our children.

If this is true, then anything that threatens the family endangers the possibility of our learning to love. And it certainly looks as if the family is seriously threatened today. One writer says that it is already "fractured" by the extraordinary changes that have taken place, and will suffer further shocks as changes occur with increasing speed and intensity.[2]

The conventional form of family life is frequently regarded as obsolescent, perhaps already obsolete. This is why so many members of the NOW generation are experimenting with other forms of living together. Varieties of communal living are being tried. Some are just living together, "without benefit of clergy," and with no commitment beyond the present.

You will not be surprised if I express some misgivings at this point. It is not that I am opposed to change, or unalterably committed to conventional arrangements. It is rather that I think the emotions involved in these relationships are profound and not to be played with. The relationships themselves are fragile; once broken, they are not easily repaired or replaced.

However, the experiments will doubtless continue. And, as a rabbi said to me recently, "We won't know who's right for another twenty years or so." That is to say, the full consequences of decisions and experiences which you enter into today may not show up for a couple of decades.

What do I mean?

The danger, as I see it, is that—with the best intentions in the world—you may engage in experiments which may spoil your capacity for entering a truly fulfilling relationship, when your chance finally comes. I can't say for sure that this will happen. But I have to warn that it may. You ought to weigh carefully the wisdom of an observation like this: "The more one abuses love, the more one craves love, and the less one is able either to feel or to obtain it."[3]

Still I have to be impressed when a thoughtful friend asks a probing question: "What if the next generation decides that there might be some more creative and authentic human relationships possible?" I have to admit the possibility that there may be such relationships. And we'll never know unless somebody tries to find them.

The key words, I would urge, are the adjectives creative and authentic. These words imply very significant human values. Whether a particular relationship is creative and authentic can only be determined relative to certain desirable goals and aspirations.

"Authentic" should mean contributing to or enhancing our true humanity. "Creative" should mean enabling us to experience our deepest human aspirations. And I am perfectly willing to have any form of family life tested by these meanings. They are very exacting.

Indeed, many conventional families fall short of these ideals. But this may not be a failure of the form so much as it is our failure to realize the potentialities of the form. It is a goal achieved only by way of discipline and integrity. And I must confess that what we regard as the conventional family looks to me like the best available relationship for growing toward this goal of creative, authentic self-realization.

Moreover, I'm willing to bet that most of the NOW generation will take this route too. They will do this, not just because it's conventional or available, but because it still looks good to them. They still see the possibility of finding fulfillment in a "nuclear family": father and mother and the desired number of children, living independently, making their own way, with only occasional reference to other members of the parents' families. Believing what I do about the three meanings we have discussed—love, sex, and marriage—I believe that this is the form of family life in which you are most likely to find the goal you seek.

I know all the negative judgments that are leveled against the nuclear family. And I have experienced most of its hazards—after all, I grew up in one, and shared another. But I'm still willing to bet that this arrangement is the one best suited to our society—including any guessable future—the one best suited to be a school for love.

I mustn't repeat all I have said about the meaning of marriage. But if commitment and fidelity are as important as I take them to be, that begins to resemble a nuclear family. I'd be the last one to deny that we may need the support and encouragement and even the counsel of our own parents and relatives, perhaps also friends and advisors, as a kind of "extended family." (Don't romanticize how welcome or helpful such advice may be at the time!) But the intimate, personal growth in our capacity to love requires the faithfulness and trust, the sense of permanence and authenticity, expressed in the union of husband and wife and their commitment to their children.

The family is a school of love for the children as well. So when we think about marriage, and the possibility of having children, we should be aware of all that is involved. Children need the same sense of trust and dependability and permanence as we do, in order to have a context in which they can learn the meaning of love.

There is a truth about children—especially babies—which isn't talked about very much but which is fundamentally important. Human babies are not born fully human but only potentially human. They have to undergo a long process of humanization. That process begins at birth, maybe even before birth. But when that baby is handed over to the parents, it still has a long way to go before it is truly human. A current writer in the field of human reproduction quotes a recognized authority to this effect: "A human baby is not born with a human nature, but rather with the capacity to become human."[4]

A baby is a bundle of potentialities that have to be elicited, directed, shaped. That's the business of the child's parents. Others will share in the process as it develops. But the initial and primary responsibility cannot be delegated to anybody else. It belongs to the parents. And with all of the inconveniences involved, I still can't see any other way to arrange things.

Parental creativity is not simply the conceiving and birthing of a child. That, indeed, may be the least demanding aspect of the whole project. An even greater creativity is required to bring out the potential humanity of the child. The name of that creativity is love—wise, caring love.

———————— ◆•◆• ◆ ————————

Here I want to say a special word to young people. You may be wondering what on earth this has to do with you at your present stage in life. Well, if you are thinking about love and marriage, you should also think about the kind of love that will be required of you if you have a family. And this is it.

If you ever have a child, what he or she will need from you more than anything else, is a quality of love that will evoke and nurture his or her own potential capacity to love. The child will need this from the moment of birth, through an incredibly complex process of living with you, until at last you can launch him or her into an independent life (when your love will still be needed, only differently).

The love of which you will have to be capable is a love freely given, frequently resisted, even rejected, but never withdrawn, always affirmed. This is what will elicit the hidden potentials of your children, and enable them in their turn to care about other people.

Incidentally, at this point I quite disagree with Fromm's understanding of paternal love. He seems to say that, while mother-love is freely given, father-love is conditional, given only if it is deserved. I disagree entirely. The father's role in the family, in child training, may be different from the mother's. But the father's love must be given just as freely as the mother's—or else it is something less than love.

That looks like a big order, doesn't it? And it is. It looks as if we all have a lot of growing to do. What I want to do here is indicate the direction in which we should be growing.

In fact, this understanding of your future relations with your children may have immediate implications for your present relations with your parents. It isn't just my paternal nosiness that leads me to ask how you get along with them. It's a simple but ironic fact of personal development: Your ability to relate well with your parents here and now will have a lot to do with your ability to become mature parents when you have to relate to your own children!

Then the relationships will be reversed. And you will

see, from that perspective, what you need to learn, just as soon as possible, from your present perspective: If a successful relation between parents and children requires wise love on the part of parents, it also requires wise love on the part of the children. This is especially true when the "children" become old enough to think of themselves as "grown up now." To ask to be treated no longer as children calls for the capacity to act with some measure of mature responsibility. (End of paternal lecture! But don't erase it too quickly. I think it's true.)

Bewildering, isn't it! Yes, and demanding too. But some of us want to assure you that it is just as rewarding as it is demanding and bewildering.

Some of us have experienced a kind of love which we never imagined was possible. This is what we hope for you. It is love committed to fidelity. It is love accepting limitations. It is love willing to suffer. It is love spending oneself for the sake of the other. It is love working through tough luck and hard times. So it is also love triumphant: love that is more than fun, it is joy; love that is more than happiness, it is fulfillment.

And we learned it in our families. That's the only place you can ever learn it.

———— ◆•◆•◆ ————

There's one speculation I can't resist putting in here. Do you suppose it is an accident that in our culture the most significant name for God is Heavenly Father? There certainly was no nuclear family in the primitive tribal civilization out of which this name came, nor even in the first-century society in which it received its deepest endorsement. But everything we have learned about ourselves simply underscores the hope that the qualities of authentic parenthood may be grounded in the very nature of the universe.

The popular psychology that dismisses such insight as a projection of a father-image is a sheer cop-out. The belief originated in a culture quite alien to ours. It has persisted through so many different cultures, that such an explanation is hardly impressive.

Is it possible that there is a reality deep within us which responds to a reality in the cosmos, to which this name, Heavenly Father, refers? There is no point in denying our human need for such a reality. And there may be good reason to suspect that it is the reality itself which evokes our need. After all, our humanity is the product of the cosmos. Cosmos produces humanity. And it may be that process and product respond to one another, identifying ultimate reality as Heavenly Father.

Can you think of a better speculation?

THE HUMAN FAMILY

Love for the whole human race would seem to be the farthest removed from love for one's immediate family. It is the difference between those whom one knows all too intimately and those whom one knows not at all or through mass media only. It is the difference between the intense, intimate feelings we share in the family and the restrained reaction to news about people on the other side of the world. It is the difference between issues in which we are personally involved and problems about which we seem to be helpless.

Yet we have it on pretty good authority that we should love our "neighbor." And in this age of the "global village," neighbor must mean anybody in the whole wide world for whom we have the slightest possible responsibility.

Actually, it seems to me that the NOW generation is very sensitive to this meaning of love. They are freer to talk about their love of mankind than their elders. A very able spokesman for this generation, writing as a university sophomore, made an interesting observation: "The word 'foreigner' has never entered youth culture."[5] He meant by this that they consider the whole body of humanity as their family: "Orphaned by a world of technology, they found in the poetic phrase 'the family of man' a very deep and meaningful allegiance."[6]

Indeed, their criticism of the establishment seems to me to be grounded in their insight that we have denied our love of humanity. They say that their elders have built a society marked by competitiveness, acquisitiveness, the lust for power, the hunger for things, the willingness to manipulate other humans for one's own benefit, nationalistic pride, and aggressiveness. And all these are betrayals of the love we really should have for our fellow human beings.

They are entirely right, of course. Many of their elders hear them and agree with them. So Archibald MacLeish writes,

> It (the student generation) is an angry generation
> but its resentment . . . is not a resentment of our
> human life but a resentment *on behalf of* human

life; not an indignation that we exist on the Earth
but that we *permit* ourselves to exist in a selfish-
ness and wretchedness and squalor which we
have the means to abolish. Resentment of this
kind is founded, can only be founded, on belief
in man. And belief in man—a return to a belief
in man—is the reality on which a new age can
be built.[7]

I suppose one measure of the gap between us is that
my generation has learned to live—even though uneasily
—with these failures. But what we have learned to live
with may be the death of this generation. So they
protest that there must be a better way. And indeed
there must.

The very eloquence and forcefulness of this protest
is a great encouragement to me. It is indeed one of
the reasons why I couldn't quite believe *Easy Rider*.
Eloquent movie that it was, it really didn't give an
honest picture.

Easy Rider presented us with only two alternative
ways of life, neither of which is desirable. And they
are not the only alternatives. If you say to me that I
have to choose between the way of irresponsible hippies
or ignorant rednecks (the only two options in the
movie), then I say you are presenting me with two
false choices. The fact is there's another alternative.

I am more than a little glad to receive support of
this interpretation from Peter Fonda himself. In an
article in *Time*, Fonda is quoted as saying, "Dennis
Hopper and I represent a complete misunderstanding of
what freedom's all about. Both concepts are untenable,

whether it's scoring and wanting to retire to Florida and ride around on your chopper, or whether it's just making money off of people."[8]

If Fonda and Hopper represent a false choice, we certainly don't want to opt for the ignorant, hateful rednecks. What then is the other alternative? It is "the dream" which one character complains "has died." But I claim that it has not died. It is alive and doing fairly well all throughout America.

It is the dream—sometimes idealistic, but more often stubbornly realistic—that we can really find a way to implement our goodwill for one another. Of course, there is hatred and prejudice and violence and greed. But there is also an impressive fund of concern, openness, and goodwill. The conflict is real and intense. The outcome is uncertain. But the dream hasn't died. In fact, there are many who are willing to act and work sacrificially for the dream's realization. And they are of several generations. Gaps close in the face of these issues.

I guess what I would hope is that youth would press its idealism and hear also the realism insisted upon by their elders. I would hope, on the other hand, that we elders who voice our realism would also affirm the idealism asserted by our youth.

———◆—◆◆◆—◆———

The fact of the case is that when love is implemented in these wide circles of nation and world, it must be concerned with the structures of society. To care about my fellow human beings in the ghetto, or in the other countries of the world, means to try to organize our ways of living together, so that everybody will get a reasonably fair deal. My concern for the families living in the depressed sections of our cities means trying to devise and support programs which will implement justice and equal opportunity in housing, in education, in employment. My goodwill toward the citizens of other countries can best be expressed in working for a world order that will alleviate the human ills that cause war and poverty.

It is very important to realize that at these points love itself cannot tell us what to do. Love does not supply the knowledge and skills required to implement itself in these wide reaches of our common life.

We need the insights and the tools of the disciplines that are devoted to these human needs: political science, economics, sociology. No amount of goodwill can be a substitute for economic reality or effective political method. Love must be implemented precisely by the means which politics, economics, and sociology tell us are viable and useful.

Of course, scholars and practitioners in these fields disagree among themselves. Men of apparently equal sincerity have conflicting ideas about how to reach common goals. This is a frequent cause of impatience to many youth of deep conviction. But I see no way to get around this except by debate and skirmish and accommodation—unless it is revolution, which will simply start another round of skirmishes.

Then when we get into the actual rough-and-tumble of politics and business, the clash of rival interests is shocking. Here decisions are made, not by polite and gentle kindness, but by the abrasive conflict of interests, by the shrewd balancing of powers. So, you may ask, if that's the name of the game, what's the relevance of love?

In the first place, I should say that love is needed as motive-power. If our dominant motives are self-interest and the will to power, then we all are goners. Honest will for the good of others and respect for their integrity must assert themselves in whatever mixture of motives gives direction to our life in society.

The will to justice is never sufficient in itself. Justice never fully embodies love. So it needs to be driven by something deeper than itself. The achievement of justice requires the motive of love.

Moreover, our own self-interest needs to be tempered by love of others. There is an aphorism out of a previous generation which will be lost unless we keep repeating it. And to lose it would cripple us. "Power corrupts; absolute power corrupts absolutely." This is true of every human being, the most idealistic among us included. And the only salvation for any or all of us is that we have some measure of love that will restrain our tendency to misuse power—with the best of intentions. We must have sufficient goodwill to recognize our self-interest, which can masquerade as the most attractive altruism.

Make no mistake, love is not too strong a word to identify what we need in order to live together in society. But love must be saved from error by wisdom, and from impotence by power. Just as power must be saved from arrogance, and wisdom from pride, by love.

A PLACE TO PRACTICE

It sounds as if what we are saying is that love is a difficult achievement. This is an unwelcome truth, usually overlooked or even denied. Sometimes we would rather believe that love is simple, it "comes naturally"—just let it happen. But the truth is that love is hard to achieve, and this seems to be true at every dimension of the experience.

When we get caught up in all the complexities of society, it seems like an insurmountable task. How on earth can I ever learn to love my neighbor? The songs and poems, the lectures and sermons, make it sound easy. "Just go out there and love everybody." But how shall we learn to balance self-interest and concern for others? How can we adjust the tensions among private benefit, the good of our peers, and the demands of general welfare? And when we have to deal with people who are hateful, suspicious, untrustworthy . . . you name it . . . love has a difficult time surviving.

Maybe we need a place to practice. Somewhere between the family and society, we need a special group —not so intimate as the family or so impersonal as society—where we can really work at the business of learning to love one another. Maybe, indeed, we need several such groups. One may serve our needs during school years, and be quite inappropriate when we have a family. So we will seek another group or groups. Some will be formed around common concerns as citizens and others around our interests as parents.

The reason why we need such groups is that society in the large is too big, too impersonal, to give us the personal support we need in our faltering efforts at loving our neighbors. We need a smaller association of people who care about one another and are willing to act as if they do care. We need a group whom we can trust—really trust—so as to be able to depend on one another. It is in such relationships that our desire to be caring persons is evoked and encouraged. We will be freer to express our concern in such a group, and strengthened by our common commitments.

The danger of such a group is that we may become self-centered, complacent, turned in upon ourselves. It is easy to think that, because we "love" one another in this congenial group, we are really fulfilling the command to love our neighbors. To succumb to such a danger is really to be defeated in this human aspiration.

The real intent of such a group is twofold. First, to build up the capacity to love. We need practice in developing the art of loving. And to be realistic about it, we need a community of like-minded people, all of whom are willing to work at developing the power to act caringly.

The second intent of such a group is to shove us out into the wider, less personal circles of society and support us in the much more difficult business of caring about our fellow citizens. Let's face it, there are a lot of unlovely people out there. So what we "practice" in the congenial circle of a loving community must be "played out" in the rough-and-tumble of society. This is where people don't seem to care about one another. This is where self-interest, class interest, vested interests of all kinds are at work. This is where power is the name of the game.

Out in these cold circles, we will need the continuing support of a community that cares about us. We need to know that we are not alone, that we have colleagues who also care, who are also doing what they have to do to express their concern wherever they are. Everyone is strengthened by the knowledge that he belongs to such a supporting community.

We return to this community . . . it may be friends in the neighborhood, political colleagues, professional or business associates, extended family, . . . we return to this community, to renew our sense of belonging to one another, of caring about one another. We review the disciplines which develop our ability to love. We "practice" some more. Then out we go again. . . . And the cycle, the rhythm, is what keeps us alive and well.

———————◆—◆◆◆—◆————————

Now let me try a thesis that you may find hard to believe. There is an organization whose original charter was to provide precisely such a series of relationships— not so intimate as the family nor so impersonal as society, but bearing a special quality of love. The name of that organization? . . . Church.

5

THE UNDERHANDED
LOVER

"He [God] was as underhand as a lover, taking advantage of a passing mood." This beautifully inelegant figure of speech has fascinated me ever since I first read it in Graham Greene's novel, *The End of the Affair.*

Greene's troubled characters, in this as in others of his novels, can't escape the sense that God is pursuing them. They would much rather be left alone, so they can enjoy their indulgences. But pleasures turn out to be less than fun, because they arouse the suspicion that God is displeased. Every "passing mood" hints at gloomy reluctant penitence, or subtly insinuates that God can really offer something much better.

You may find this insight quite new or unconvincing. So let's turn it around and look at it from another perspective. The other side of the truth is that every profound human experience suggests the reality of God. Every human grace reflects his goodness. Every frustration, every anxiety points to his responsive love.

In terms of our present study, I want to put it this way. Our deepest insights into and experiences of love are signals of the reality of a God who is love. Our capacity to love is the sign of our origin. Our need for love is the mark of our Maker. Our inability to love is an indication that we have fallen away from our built-in purposes. Our frustrations point to the divine intention to restore our weakened powers. The intersection between our need and our impotence looks suspiciously like a cross.

Everything depends on whether we can receive the signals and interpret them. I have suggested that part of our difficulty is that a lot of different people are sending out conflicting messages in our culture. If there is any authentic signal anywhere, it may be jammed or distorted by all the others being emitted. And our own receiving isn't always objective and disinterested, by any standard. Somewhere, we must pick up a key which will enable us to make some sense out of all we are hearing, we must find a clue which will help us interpret the signals. Let's look.

READING THE SIGNALS

We defined love as the capacity to give ourselves to another person or other persons. People need people. We need to be able to relate to others with openness and trust and honesty. But our ability to do so is limited and frustrated. And when we are honest, we recognize that these limitations are within ourselves.

To be freed up for love, we must be loved, freely, for ourselves, in such a manner as to awaken and heal our own frustrated powers. But such love is not easily given, since others are as limited as we are. Nor is it easily received, since it is difficult for us to open ourselves.

We need to love. But we need to be loved so that we can love. If this sounds like a vicious circle, it is. It is precisely such a futile circling of desire and need that most of us experience. Our anxiety is that we are not loved. Our frustration is that we cannot love.

There "just happens" to be a faith which meets us at exactly this point of need with a remarkable assertion. You are loved. Before you ever knew it, or cared—and even if you still don't know or care, you are loved with exactly the kind of freely-offered love you need, designed to evoke your power to love, to free up your frustrated capacity for love.

———— ◆•◆•◆ ————

We considered sexuality as the longing for wholeness experienced by male and female. Our maleness seeks union with femaleness. Our femaleness seeks union with maleness. And in this union our human wholeness is realized. We interpreted marriage as the commitment to such a union, full of sacramental and creative possibilities. Yet we had to admit that wholeness is a difficult achievement, blocked by all sorts of personal hangups.

These thoughts aroused echoes of a dialog in Eden. There came back to our minds stories sceptically remembered: stories about Adam and Eve, a promised oneness, something gone wrong, a mess made of the whole project.

Then another echo: the favorite name for God, frequently profaned by our own mixed-up family relations, challenged by proudly championed doubts and questions. But maybe it's a signal of something cosmically true: Heavenly Father. Maybe there is something to this business of love. Maybe there is a promise of realization and fulfillment that we can trust.

***

The will to love draws us out to our fellow human beings. Their need evokes our concern. And an ancient command to love our neighbor seems to express our deepest desire. But we find this is very difficult. We can manage to love certain people rather easily. But parents? Children? People we don't like, whom we can't trust, whose motives we suspect? You can easily make a list of people whom you find it very hard to love—if not impossible.

How do we get out of this impasse? You can shrug it off as if it doesn't matter. But you know it does. This command, or something like it, is quite fundamental to our human family. You can be sentimental, and talk about love as if it were "natural" and easy. But it won't test out. The realities are too tough for us. And the dawning of the age of Aquarius won't swing it. The fault—and the cure—is not in the stars but in ourselves. Something has to reach us at the level of our own need and impotence.

There "just happens" to be a faith which continues to send out strange signals. The command to love comes from a God who already loves you. What he demands he wants also to give. And he wants to give precisely in order to enable you to give what you need to give— your love for and to others.

Any signals coming through? That your need to love may be a sign that you owe your being to one whose nature is to love? That your inability to love calls forth the searching, sacrificial response of one whose whole will is to love?

There "just happens" to be a faith which picks up all these signals and makes sense of them. The "key" to reading the signals is not a doctrine to be believed, or a book to be studied, or a world view to be adopted, but a Person to be trusted. You know, of course, that I am talking about Jesus Christ. Are you willing to see where he might lead us?

"GOD IS LOVE"[1]

Christianity really has a strange notion about God. That is, it would be strange, if it hadn't become so conventional. Actually, I think there's nothing like it in all the religions of the world. With all your present fondness for esoteric and exotic ideas out of the East, you mustn't be misled by apparent similarities. I'll just bet you won't find anything quite like the next several paragraphs in any other religion but Christianity. (And what similarities we do find, we discover only after we have been given the clue in Jesus Christ.)

"God is love." Most of you have heard it most of your life. It may conjure up all sorts of sentimental, abstract ideas. But it is neither abstract nor sentimental. It is concrete, specific, realistic.

When the New Testament says that God is love, it means, "God actively loves you. God is actually giving himself for you in love. He is sacrificially spending his powers, just to communicate to you one basic fact: 'I really care about you. The one thing that matters to me is your well-being, your real humanity.' "

I have heard this verse interpreted to mean that God is a relationship. This is hardly what the writer was trying to say. He was affirming that God is a Person giving himself in loving action on behalf of the human beings he loves. God is not a relationship (whatever that might mean). God is a Lover, a Loving Person.

Now I know that there are a dozen implications hidden in such a statement . . . profound inquiries that we simply can't go into here. Just as I made no effort to deal exhaustively with issues in political science and sociology, so now I dare not become involved in theological and philosophical issues which are very important but would distract us from our central concern.[2]

We must stay with the love theme. That means taking seriously the biblical affirmation: "God is love." God is, always and everywhere, actively and persistently giving himself to his human creatures in love. His primary purpose is to persuade us that he really cares about us, and win us to a commitment to this reality. He knows that our humanity depends on such persuasion and such commitment. And it is the fulfillment of our humanity that he wills . . . actively and deliberately wills.

———◆◆◆◆———

We have said that Jesus is the "key" which enables us to sort out our experiences of love and interpret them in this extraordinary way. That God is love is surely the burden of his teaching—even if he himself never said it in exactly those words.

God is like a shepherd, he said, one of whose sheep has somehow got away from the rest: he beds down the flock safely, and goes out to look for the lost one. Or again, God looks for us with all the energy of a woman who has misplaced her life-savings, and turns the house upside down looking for them.

Or he put it another way—and here he touches us most closely. God is like a father whose younger son rebelled and got into trouble. But the father never gives up on the boy. And when his son finally comes to his senses, the father runs out to meet him and welcome him home.[3]

But Jesus did as good as he said. He was sensitive and gentle with the exploited and abused. He was open to the morally disreputable. When challenged by the respectable members of the Establishment, Jesus simply said, "I go to these people because they need me. That's the way God is." The so-called respectable people needed him too. He tried to reach them, but they

couldn't recognize their need. And hardly anyone—
then or now—understood what he was really trying to
demonstrate: This is the way God is.

A few, however, took him seriously. And they came
to believe that Jesus is God's love in action. If you ask
how can we know what God is like, they add, we can
only reply that he is like Jesus. The argument is not
logical but circular—and it packs a lot of power.

It is precisely this aggressive, outgoing, self-giving
quality which characterizes God's love for us. This is
the uniquely Christian affirmation. And Jesus Christ is
the sign and symbol of it all.

Thoughtful Christians have always had an uncanny
sense that God is actually out to get us. He's after us at
every twist and turn of our life. We are likely to meet
him at the most unexpected places.

We may be going along, minding our own business,
and all of a sudden a stab of affection for someone
or concern for an abused person reminds us that God
is around. It may be a sudden sense of beauty or joy
that hints at a divine goodness (C. S. Lewis was "Surprised by Joy"). An unexpected moment of ecstasy
carries overtones of a cosmic mystery. (A wife turns
to her husband, and in a muffled voice, says, "Hey, that
was a little bit profound.") Or it may be a dark moment
of anxiety, of uneasiness, maybe despair, in which we
cry for resources greater than those we have at hand,
and something—someone?—responds.

Many a Christian has had a strange feeling that when
he finally found God, it was because God had been
looking for him all the time. Pascal put it like this: "We

could not have found you, if you had not already found us."

In your personal experiences of love, frustrated or fun, God is trying to reach you. Are you willing to read your experiences as signals of a deeper love which is seeking to bring you to real fulfillment?

———◆━◆━◆━◆———

There's another word for this divine quality—a lovely word, a little old-fashioned, but you shouldn't lose it out of your vocabulary (or your experience). It is "grace."

It was Paul who put this word at the center of the Christian vocabulary. He was in an odd spot. He was a Jew using the Greek language to communicate brand-new Christian ideas and experiences. He had to grab every usable word within reach, in order to express what no one had ever had to say before. That's why—plus the fact that he was a first-century man—he's so difficult to read. But it's also why he's so stimulating.

Paul simply couldn't get over his unbelievable discovery that God really does love his human creatures. This, he said, is what Jesus Christ is all about. He is the embodiment of divine grace. "Grace," then, is simply another word for the surprising, unexpected, undeserved love of God.

The quality of surprise and joy in our discovery of grace is expressed in an old American folk hymn. I remember the fun of learning that Arlo Guthrie, the folk singer, and I have one thing in common: "Amazing Grace" is our favorite hymn. Then I realized why it had figured so prominently in the movie *Alice's Restaurant*, which had impressed me deeply.

Alice's Restaurant tells an appealing, sympathetic, frequently hilarious, but basically sad story. It portrays the way of life pursued by a group of young adults. A compassionate couple has taken over an old, deconsecrated church, which has become a sort of home and community center for the young people. Their life consists largely of uncommitted drifting, pot smoking, and casual sex.

This community, gathered in their church for a holiday celebration, lounging around in a drugged euphoria, sing that beautiful old American hymn.

> Amazing grace! how sweet the sound
> That saved a wretch like me!
> I once was lost, but now am found,
> Was blind, but now I see.

The words were familiar enough to me. Well-sung and well-staged, they were deeply moving. But was this rendition, in this setting, really expressing the intended meaning of the words? Were these young adults, high on grass, indolently sexy, experiencing the kind of grace the hymn really celebrates?

I had to conclude that they were not—not really. There was a "grace" among them, to be sure. It was an attractive, appealing camaraderie. But it lacked depth and durability. Subsequent events revealed that they really didn't care about each other, and the group was destroyed. That was the essential sadness of the story.

But this human grace—however disfigured—reflects a divine grace. Our human caring is the image of the divine caring. Our need for each other is the mark of our making—our Maker built this in. Our failure to achieve the kind of love we long for evokes the hope that the one who made us will not let us go. And the hope is met by a promise . . . he won't. So we encounter a divine love, freely given, never withdrawn, sacrificially affirmed. It really is "amazing."

THE STRANGEST "NO"

A subtle irony has been lurking in this discussion. The fact is that all of us reject God's approach . . . and some of us never do get 'round to accepting it.

This surely has to be the strangest "no" in human utterance. We turn away from God's advances. He offers us exactly what we need to satisfy our deepest longings . . . and we say, "Thanks, but no thanks."

There are reasons enough, very human reasons. We'd rather manage things ourselves. We are reluctant to admit that we need anybody, other than a little help from our friends. We like to hold on to our self-styled autonomy (an illusion, but we cling to it). And we're not about to give up the direction of our own lives to anybody . . . not even God . . . especially not God.

The irony is that these very human reasons for rejecting God result in the spoiling of our humanity. The community in *Alice's Restaurant* is destroyed. The hippie commune in *Easy Rider* starves on its own illusions. And the riders themselves explode in a burst of violence that makes us hate their killers. *Hair* salutes freedom and love, but reduces many human relations to sheer animalism. Sex without love is nothing but *Carnal Knowledge.*

The most dramatic illustration of the way in which our humanity is spoiled by our rejection of God lies precisely in the area of human relations which we have been examining, our sexuality. Has it ever occurred to you that maybe our sexuality is not now what it was originally intended to be? In fact nothing about us, as we now are, embodies fully the original intention that was written into our being. And nowhere is this more awkwardly true than with respect to our sexual powers.

Why should this be true? Precisely because our sexuality is so profound a part of our humanity. When we were made human, we were made male and female human. According to an ancient story, our sexuality is mentioned in the same sentence with our divine image.[4] And in the wisdom of the race, as in sophisticated storytelling, sentences like that don't just happen.

Incidentally, in the effort to state a Christian understanding of our sexuality, we have to resort to story. We may do this without apology. Whenever serious thinkers try to get at the heart of our human condition, they have to go beyond discursive language and resort to myth. The Greeks did this. Look at what Freud did with the story of Oedipus. Rollo May is forced to similar interpretations again and again. The deeper we probe into our humanity, the more complex and profound we appear to be. And at last, we have to drop logical language, and resort to storytelling, to figurative and poetic language, perhaps even to myth.

It is the story of Adam and Eve which dramatizes our human condition. The divine intention for his creatures was their good, their fulfillment. Their sexuality was part of this intention.

Our profound longing for wholeness is mythically expressed by the poetic assertion that Eve was made from Adam's rib. Then follows one of the most beautiful insights in religious literature. When Adam sees Eve, it is as if a shudder of recognition runs through him. He exclaims, "This at last is bone of my bones, and flesh of my flesh." And the promise is that the two —in their fidelity to one another—shall become one.[5] Each is part of the essential being of the other. Their wholeness is realized only in union.

By the way . . . don't pass too lightly over the remarkable assertion that the two shall become one. (At least, this was the way Jesus read it.) This story had its origin in the prehistoric beginnings of the Hebrew tribes. It was recorded during a period of their history when polygamy was not unacceptable. Yet out of this primitive origin, this mixed history, comes a profound affirmation of monogamy. Human beings find their wholeness in the union of one male and one female. This extraordinary insight deserves profound reflection.

Then look what happened!

Adam and Eve had everything going for them. But they tried to assert their own autonomy. They were determined to do their own thing. And they blew it.

(This is the story of our life. As one of my great professors used to say, "My name is Adam." To which my

wife always responds, "Just call me Eve." And somewhere C. S. Lewis puts it with a characteristic twist:
"We dance Adam's dance backwards.")

When their relationship with God is spoiled, everything else begins to go wrong. Now, for the first time,
they are embarrassed by their nudity.[6] Indeed, when
God confronts them, he is shocked by their fig leaf
cover-up. He asks, with a pathos seldom matched in
literature, "Who told you you were naked?"[7] It is clear
that he hadn't. Their shame was the consequence of
their folly. They had spoiled the intended beauty of
their sexuality.

Then everything goes wrong. Their innocence destroyed, they have to start making their own history.
And what happens? Murder! In fact, man kills his own
brother.[8] And the human story is on its way. "So it
goes."[9]

Now we are getting to the heart of the matter. This
ancient tale is concerned not only with our sexuality
but with our total human condition. When we dislodge
the center of our life, we become eccentric. This in turn
spoils all of our human relations.

Somewhere I have read a comment of a wise Jesuit
teacher who remarked, "Given enough time, everything
human will go wrong." Many people aren't used to
hearing talk like that. They are inclined to take a rather
rosy view of human nature. But here is an insight
shocking in its honesty, clear-eyed in its realism. Therefore, I would add, it is the only view which can be
authentic in its hope.

There's something desperately wrong with us. It is

deeper than psychology, more pervasive than sociology. It lies at the core of our being. Could it be this primordial denial of our true origin?

———— ◆—•◉•—◆ ————

The seriousness of our human condition is matched only by the seriousness of God's caring. Here Christianity makes its most shocking claim—unparalleled in all the pre-Christian religions of the world, and only dimly guessed even in religions that have felt the influence of Christianity.

God does not turn away from us, or against us, because of our folly and self-centeredness. He has made us; he ran the risk of giving us our responsible freedom. And he wants to save us from the consequences of our misuse of his endowment. So he continues to seek us, to try to reach us. He becomes "an underhanded lover...."

Creative love becomes suffering love. The love of God is not placid, safe, sure of itself. The divine love is agonized, taking risks—even the risk of rejection.

So love assumes the form of a cross. And this, at last, is what Jesus Christ is all about. The Christian faith at its best has always tried to say what is ultimately, I suppose, beyond words. The supreme expression of God's love for us is Christ's death on a cross.

This event in history discloses what is eternally true in the life of God. One New Testament author speaks of "the Lamb slain from the foundation of the world." And Pascal comments that Christ is in agony until the end of the world.

How can we say this? It's easier not to try. So the philosopher dismisses it with cruel logic. Popular religion either bypasses it or reduces it to crude butchery. And good-natured youth, with uneasy elders, live with sentimental illusions. So the realities of our human need are hidden and unanswered. The resources of divine love are unrecognized and denied.

But if we take seriously the meaning of love, we are drawn at last to the cross. Cruciform love is love at its deepest and truest and most powerful. If we open ourselves to this deed, to this Person, we will be shocked out of our sentimentality. Our need for love will be met by this freely-given love. And the restorative power of divine love will evoke our capacity for caring and giving.

Our tragic "no" is not the last word. God's "yes" is still spoken: Adam and Eve . . . John and Mary . . . you are mine. . . . Don't try to be something else, something you can never be. . . . Be what you are intended to be. . . . My man or woman, therefore truly human.

FAITH AS LIBERATION

There is another unexpected facet to our human "no"-saying. The "no" which we utter to God is indeed the deepest tragedy of our existence. But the freedom to utter this "no" is the deepest mark of our humanity. That we *do* say "no" is tragic. That we *can* say "no" is the glory of our being human.

In the beauty of our freedom and in the wonder of God's grace, lies the possibility of our "no" being transformed to a "yes." And this "yes" is life-affirming, life-changing, life-directing. It restores our human-ness.

God's grace is intended to evoke our "yes."

You can say "yes" to yourself, accepting the reality of what you are. You can do this because God says "yes" to you—just as you are. No more make-believe, masks, or false appearances. Just "yes."

You can say "yes" to God, accepting the acceptance which he extends, the direction which he offers. No more game-playing, pretending he isn't there, or that he will make up the losses. Just "yes."

You can say "yes" to life, to the future. There's a good deal about it which isn't too pretty or too promising. But God is bigger than history. His purposes have a longer run than our performances. And if we take hold of those purposes, nothing can really hurt us. He is what life is all about. Just "yes."

This yes-saying is what Christianity means by faith. I am sorry to have to resort to another theological term, but it's both useful and necessary.

Necessary because faith is so frequently misunderstood. It does not mean believing something for which you have no proof. That's a caricature resorted to by people who really should know better. For thoughtful Christians, faith has never meant blind belief.

Useful because faith is a word which has become central to our whole Christian way of thinking about life. Again it was Paul who put this word into our Christian vocabulary. He practically had to make up the whole vocabulary, as it was. And this was the best term he could find to identify . . . *saying "yes" with everything you have.*

Faith is known to the most careful students of the New Testament as an act of the whole person. Faith is our response to God's action. We pull ourselves together —or we let ourselves be drawn together—and we say "yes" to God's affirmation of us.

It has always been useful to me to think of faith as involving all of our powers, which I summarize as will, intellect, and emotion. Faith involves us in decisions of will, efforts of intellect, and surges of emotion. There's no saying "which comes first." Each person responds in ways appropriate to himself. But it is to be hoped that the whole person will be involved. God wants all of you to get into the act.

Faith is a decision of your will. Rollo May offers a succinct definition of will which is very helpful: "The capacity to organize one's self so that movement in a certain direction or toward a certain goal may take place."[10] Faith, then, is pulling yourself together, organizing your powers, so that you may move toward the goal which you imagine Jesus would want you to achieve. This goal is not to be thought of so much in terms of moralistic striving as in terms of the kind of person you are, the quality of your life.

And it is not as if you claim to have reached the goal. Faith is a process, as life is a process. Faith puts you in motion toward a goal. Motion is not constant or uninterrupted. It is apt to be zigzag, moving by fits and starts, perhaps even suffering setbacks. What is important is the direction.

108

So faith is pulling yourself together, committing yourself to a purpose, setting a direction for your life. And for Christian faith all of this is defined in relation to Jesus Christ.

You can't be at this very long before you have to start using your head. Why should we take Jesus so seriously? What's so special about him? And how do I know what he wants of me?

You really can't answer these questions with the kind of religious resources most of you have been given up to now. Kid stuff is no longer good enough. Somewhere along the line, if you're going to bother to be a Christian, you may as well be a well informed one.

It is sad to see intelligent students rejecting Christianity for unintelligent reasons. Even as highly a trained man as Bertrand Russell did this. Reading his *Why I Am Not a Christian,* I can only groan that, wise and admirable as he was in so many ways, he apparently never took the trouble to learn what intelligent Christians believe and teach nowadays.

There is a lot of such lack of information on the academic scene, both among students and teachers. Indeed, in the church itself, there is widespread avoidance of intellectual issues among people who have never rejected conventional faith, but have never bothered to think about it either.

I'm inviting you to consider an alternative: the willing use of intelligence to understand what the Christian faith is all about. You don't become a Christian simply by the use of intellect. But you become a mature Christian, by being willing to add intellectual excellence to your total experience of Christ.

Faith catches up our feelings too. Why have we been so suspicious of religious feelings? Maybe some of them have been phoney. But do we have to go to the other extreme and squeeze all the fun out of religion?

Certainly, in our day there is much emphasis on the release of feelings. We are trying to get freed up by resorting to various psychological and group practices.

Just as certainly, if we take Jesus Christ seriously, it's going to stir our feelings. Joy has been a big word in Christian writings. Come to think of it, love is not exactly devoid of feelings either.

There's a deeper level of emotion involved too. We all carry within us the feelings of anxiety, loneliness, fear, hostility. These need to be eased up, maybe even purged. Christian experience is no cheap psychiatry. But when it is authentic, it gets at some of these gnawing feelings. And the deep potentialities of trust and honesty and caring, these can be released in the growing experience of faith.

The dark powers which spoil life can be understood and healed by our faith, in response to God's grace. The bright and healthful powers which make life good can be released and freed up by the divine grace which is met by our faith.

So faith looks very much like love. Acts like it. Feels like it too.

What is even more surprising is that faith feels like freedom. And it is. The life of faith means liberation to become what you are intended to be, what you deeply want to be.

Underscore "become." Liberation is a becoming. Freedom is a process. You don't become liberated overnight (only unbuttoned?). You grow into genuine liberty. Freedom, like love, is an achievement. But if faith means "getting it all together," "getting your head on straight," then faith is essential to freedom.

You can be freed up to become yourself. Because now you can know who you are supposed to be, what you have to work with, what hangups you have to overcome, and what resources you can call in.

You can be liberated from the manipulation and coercion of a commercialized, competitive culture. Now you have a sense of direction, an inner drive. Now that you know who you are, you can do your own thing.

The stereotypes of maleness and femaleness are relaxed now. You are free to be a real person, to become a whole person. Male does not dominate female, nor female manipulate male. Both together discover their real humanity.

You are freed from the bondage of permissiveness. When "anything goes," nothing really matters. Permissiveness destroys meaning. And meaningless existence becomes boring. And boredom is deadly.

But now you have a meaning to your life—to realize the potentialities that God has given you, to be his person. So you are released into a glad obedience. And because what you obey is really what you are made for, obedience yields joy, excitement.

Idealistic? Yes. But very real. Just ask anybody who has opened himself to authentic faith, and he will tell you that he has discovered the secret of liberation.

God, the Liberator!

Oh, freedom!

That's what he wanted for us all the time. No wonder it seems so right.

A SORT OF EXTENDED FAMILY

Love requires community. The hermit is an eccentric. People need people. Even beyond our families, we need ties of trust and concern with other human beings. I think you know this without my having to say it too many times.

But the human family is a big crowd. It can be lonely —or vicious—out there. So, I have said, we need to be associated with smaller groups of people, with whom we can experience special relationships of love. And I barely, almost hesitantly, mentioned that there is a group designed specifically for that purpose . . . the church.

I can hear you gasp, "You've got to be kidding!" But I'm not at all. I know very well that churches don't look as if they serve such a purpose. But institutions are like people: we fall short of our intentions. Our failures may contradict, but they need not destroy the purposes for which we were made. So the church, whatever it may look like, is really intended to be a community of people whose relations with one another are marked by a special quality of love.

Here's another of those truths which can be turned around and looked at from a different perspective. Wherever a special quality of caring for one another is developed in a group, there is "a church" or a reasonable facsimile. It is both possible and desirable for you to enter into a relationship with other people, in which you learn to care very much about each other. It may be a commune, a community organization, a club—almost anything. When there develops genuine caring, honest trust, and when you learn to act in trustful love for one another, there you have something which approaches what the New Testament means by "church."

However, from the Christian point of view, "church" has a more specific connotation. A church is a community of people who have learned about love from Jesus Christ. We have experienced God's love through Christ. This common experience draws us into a community in which we discover a special love for one another. We know that we have opened ourselves to the grace of God, therefore we are free to open ourselves to one another. We know that we are loved by God, so we are enabled to love one another. The church is intended to be a community of love.

It is a place to practice. That is, in the smaller community we are freed up, by our common faith and experience, to care about one another. As we experience the love of God more deeply, we are given greater freedom. In our relations with one another, we grow in strength and power to love.

But what we practice in this community is to be exercised in society. We are thrust out from the church to express our love in the world. Yet all the while, we know we are supported in our efforts by the loving community to which we belong. We all are trying to do the same thing—care about our fellow humans, and express that concern in the struggles and structures of society.

What bothers me is not only that we fail to live up to this ideal, but that we have largely lost the vision itself. And because we don't really understand what the church is supposed to be, it becomes a complacent club, or a society of uptight moralists, or a political lobby. In any case, the real intention of the church is lost, and we are robbed of something we seriously need—a place to practice real love for one another.

———◆◆◆◆———

Only recently it has occurred to me that there's another way of saying this. In our discussion of the family, we noted that some scholars fear that the nuclear family cannot meet the demands imposed by present and future social changes. And I admit that the nuclear family does run the risk of becoming isolated, turned in on itself.

The single family needs the support of caring persons outside the immediate circle. These may be relatives or friends or chosen associates. They offer an added dimension of affection, experience, and support to the members of the family. They become what is called an "extended family."

As I was talking about such matters with some friends, I realized that this is exactly what the church is supposed to be . . . a sort of extended family. We don't necessarily form a commune. Most of us cherish the privacy and integrity of our own families. But we have many different relationships in the church which are very important to us in our personal and family life.

Admittedly, what usually happens is that within the larger congregation, we find smaller associations which give the kind of support and strength we need. Most congregations are themselves too big to accomplish this. But the total congregation makes possible the other groupings, and sustains their life. So we learn to trust one another and to care about each other. We are not isolated. We stand together. We support and sustain one another in more ways than we can easily say.

It really isn't my intention to sell you on the church right now. But I'd be less than honest if I failed to say that here's a resource for learning to love that some of us have found indispensable.

One difficulty of the church is that it is made up of so many different kinds of people. But that is also one of its merits. The average church is a cross section of the kind of society you have to learn to live in. And here's your chance to get some experience under relatively (!) favorable conditions. I won't pretend that everything is, or will be, smooth sailing. But that isn't true anywhere, is it? What is true in the church is that, every once in a while, we have discovered relationships of trust and concern and understanding. And we have been strengthened by all this.

Of course, such relationships can be formed quite apart from any organized church. What I want to suggest, I suppose, is basically two-sided. First, you need such relationships to a group of trusted friends, who will really care about you and for whom you can care. And second, there is an organization which has exactly this in mind. It may just fit your needs.

Perhaps even more basic, I would say, is the insight that this need is rooted in the way you have been made. And the one who made you wants to provide for your needs. He has tried to do this through Jesus Christ. And it is certainly no accident that the church is known as "the body of Christ." The business of the church is to help you become the kind of person you are meant to be, to share both the achievement and its means with others, and to work out the implications for this in society.

This interpretation of the church may be rather new to you. And I guess it is somewhat unconventional. So you may ask me what is the basis for such a suggestion. I would reply that it is my understanding of what the New Testament means by church.

This is no place to expound such a doctrine. Let me simply say that it is my impression that whenever the New Testament speaks most deeply and intensively about human beings loving one another, it does so in the context of the Christian community. The command to love our neighbor is clear enough. And that means our fellow humans in society. But there seems to be another dimension of love which is shared by those who have experienced the love of God through Jesus Christ.

There are three passages which document this thesis.

Let me put them in a note and you can do what you please with them.[11] But I cannot resist adding that in my judgment the widespread disregard of this insight is robbing most church members of a resource we all need. If we are really to learn to love one another we need a place to practice, an extended family in which we can expand our powers of love.

The irony, of course, is that the church has never really lived up to this high view of its function. Right in the New Testament there is evidence of dissension, rivalries, arguments, misunderstandings. We are simply too human to live up to our full humanity! And the church is no exception.

But what we need is not a perfect community. What we need is an association of people we can trust, who can care about one another, who can support one another in our attempts to live well in society. God has tried to provide us with one. The organization itself may fall short of its intended purpose. But God can help us find other ways of meeting this need.

We can be the body of Christ, a community of love, bound together in commitment to our Leader, deeply involved with one another, and honestly active to do his work in the world.

117

PRELUDE:
LOVE AND HOPE

"Love hopes all things." That's what the Bible says.

What does it mean? That we have to be good-natured optimists? That we just keep telling ourselves that everything will turn out all right in the end?

Not many of you are going to accept such a grinning optimism, even though there is a sort of facile naïveté about some youthful sentiments. The inclination of many sensitive and concerned people—both young and not-so-young—is to be pretty hopeless about the future, or at least sceptical. The issues confronting our society are enormous. The rigidity and indifference of the Establishment threaten to render the system incapable of responding to these issues. So the hope that love may win out, over enormous odds, seems pretty dim.

"Love conquers all" runs another aphorism out of our past. Is this what we ought to hope? Well, it depends on how you interpret the saying.

One of the great novels of recent years (1957) was *By Love Possessed*, by James Gould Cozzens. Ironically, it opens and closes with scenes in which the protagonist stands before a mantle clock bearing the Latin motto *Ommia vincit amor*. The words are decorated with the classic figures of a partially undraped nymph, a peeping shepherd, and above them shy Cupid with his poised bow and arrow.

Is this what we are to believe in?

The novel assures us that such naïveté is foolish and even destructive. The characters are themselves possessed by what commonly passes for some variety of "love." But in every significant instance, their "love" conquers nothing at all. In fact, it fails to sustain them in any important event of their lives.

Frankly, I think the author is exactly right. What we customarily take to be "love" doesn't conquer anything. It usually turns out to be quite destructive. So what can we mean when we say, "Love hopes all things"?

First, let's read the whole statement in a modern translation. "There is nothing love cannot face; there is no limit to its faith, its hope, and its endurance."[1] That says it better. Love can face anything with assurance and trust—even its own defeat.

What, then, is the basis for love's hope?

Simply this: God is love.

There are many ways of making such an affirmation. The universe is not indifferent to human values, but is on the side of love. The very nature of reality supports and sustains the integrity of love. The ultimate reality is not matter or mathematics, but a divine purpose to guarantee the supremacy of love. God's power is directed toward one supreme goal: to persuade us to care for one another and to ensure the final triumph of such a caring way of life.

If God is love, then love must ultimately triumph over every force and event which challenges it. History may not document the supremacy of love. History, indeed, may simply illustrate man's inhumanity to man. Historically, it may look as if we not only act hatefully to one another, but we seem to get away with it. Love seems to be defeated repeatedly in human affairs. One doesn't have to be much of a sceptic to say, "Hateful power conquers all."

But God is not defeated by our historical follies and tragedies. He, by definition, will have the last word! If God is really God, he will ultimately triumph. His purposes will ultimately be realized. And those who commit themselves to these purposes will share in this final assertion.

Time may have a stop. The human story may come to a gasping conclusion. But that's not the end for God. His purposes look beyond time and history. And his purpose is love. Therefore, if love does not in fact conquer all, love will outlast everything else. It was our same writer who said, "Love will never come to an end."[2]

This, then, is our hope. And once it has really taken hold of us, we can handle anything.

"In a word, there are three things that last for ever: faith, hope, and love; but the greatest of them all is love."[3]

NOTES

Chapter 1. How Does Love Happen?

1. James Joyce, *Ulysses* (New York: Random House, 1914).

2. *Saturday Review,* July 24, 1971, p. 33.

3. Ibid.

4. Erich Fromm, *The Art of Loving: An Enquiry into the Nature of Love* (New York: Harper & Row, 1956), p. 26.

5. Rollo May, *Love and Will* (New York: W. W. Norton & Co., 1969), p. 283.

6. Ibid., chapter 12.

7. Cf. Fromm, op. cit., pp. 9, 18, 20-21; May, op. cit., pp. 75, 111-12, 145.

8. Richard Brautigan, *Trout Fishing in America* (New York: Dell, 1967), p. 9.

9. Eldridge Cleaver, "'The Christ' and His Teachings," *Soul on Ice* (New York: McGraw-Hill, 1968), pp. 31-39.

10. May, op. cit., pp. 317, 319. Used by permission.

Chapter 2. Love Among the Ruins

1. *Time* magazine, July 11, 1969, pp. 61ff.

2. Leopold Tyrmand, "Reflections: Permissiveness and Rectitude," *Notebooks of a Dilettante* (New York: Macmillan, 1970). Copyright © 1970 by Leopold Tyrmand. Essay originally published in *The New Yorker*, Feb. 28, 1970; see p. 94. Used by permission of The Macmillan Company.

3. George Wald, Harvard University, in a speech frequently reproduced and quoted.

4. Margaret Mead, *Saturday Review*, Jan. 10, 1970, p. 113.

5. John Hyde Preston, "Love Among the Ruins," *Harper's Monthly Magazine*, July 1934, p. 182.

6. Ibid., p. 189.

7. Richard F. Hettlinger, *Living with Sex: The Student's Dilemma* (New York: Seabury Press, 1966), p. 8. Copyright 1966 by The Seabury Press, Inc. Used by permission.

8. Idem.

9. "The increase in the incidence of premarital coitus, and the similar increase in the incidence of premarital petting, constitute the greatest changes which we have found between the patterns of sexual behavior in the older and younger generation of American females. . . . Practically all of this increase has occurred in the generation that was born in the first decade of the present century and, therefore, in the generation which had had most of its premarital experience in the late teens and in the 1920's following the First World War. The later generations appear to have accepted the new pattern and maintained or extended it." Alfred C. Kinsey, *Sexual Behavior in the Human Female*, pp. 298-99. Used by permission of Indiana University, Bloomington, Ind. Cf. also Albert Ellis, *Sex Without Guilt* (New York: Grove Press, 1965), p. 26: "All the facts at our disposal show that premarital relations have been unusually widespread for the last half century." Used by permission.

10. Rollo May, *Love and Will* (New York: W. W. Norton & Co., 1969), p. 39. Used by permission.

11. Penelope Gilliatt, *The New Yorker*, June 13, 1970, p. 103.

Chapter 3. Love and Sex: Beyond Morality

1. Albert Ellis, *Sex Without Guilt* (New York: Grove Press, 1965), pp. 170. Used by permission.

2. Ibid., p. 176.

3. Ibid., pp. 47, 71, 69, 137.

4. Robert T. Francoeur, *Utopian Motherhood: New Trends in Human Reproduction* (Garden City, N. Y.: Doubleday, 1970), p. 243. Note, however, that he goes on to add, "Despite this confusion, there is a sense in which we can and must affirm that sex is fun." Idem.

5. Cf. Rollo May, *Love and Will* (New York: W. W. Norton & Co., 1969), pp. 145-53, 311, 313; Erich Fromm, *The Art of Loving: An Enquiry into the Nature of Love* (New York: Harper & Row, 1956), pp. 33-38, 52-57.

6. Eldridge Cleaver, *Soul on Ice* (New York: McGraw-Hill, 1968), pp. 176ff.

7. May, op. cit., chapter 2. Cf. also p. 314: "The love act is distinguished by being procreative; and ... this is the basic symbol of love's creativity."

8. Norman Mailer, "The White Negro," *The Beat Generation and the Angry Young Men*, ed. Gene Feldman and Max Gartenberg (New York: Citadel Press, 1957), pp. 352, 354.

9. *Time* magazine, Oct. 31, 1969, p. 67.

10. William J. Lederer and Don D. Jackson, *Mirages of Marriage* (New York: W. W. Norton & Co., 1968), p. 13.

11. Leopold Tyrmand, "Reflections: Permissiveness and Rectitude," *Notebook of a Dilettante* (New York: Macmillan, 1970). Copyright © 1970 by Leopold Tyrmand. Essay originally published in *The New Yorker*, Feb. 28, 1970; see p. 96. Used by permission of The Macmillan Company.

12. As reported in the *San Francisco Examiner*, Feb. 17, 1970, p. 15.

13. Cf. Denis de Rougemont's somewhat more serious judgment: "Once we ask ourselves what is involved in choosing a man or a woman *for the rest of one's life*, we see that to choose is to wager." *Love in the Western World* (New York: Fawcett World), p. 317.

Chapter 4.   Circles of Love

1. Erich Fromm, *The Art of Loving: An Enquiry into the Nature of Love* (New York: Harper & Row, 1956), p. 47.

2. Alvin Toffler, *Future Shock* (New York: Random House, 1970), especially pp. 211-30.

3. Leopold Tyrmand, "Reflections: Permissiveness and Rectitude," *Notebooks of a Dilettante* (New York: Macmillan, 1970). Copyright © 1970 by Leopold Tyrmand. Essay originally published in *The New Yorker,* Feb. 28, 1970; see p. 92. Used by permission of The Macmillan Company.

4. Ashley Montagu, quoted in Robert T. Francoeur, *Utopian Motherhood: New Trends in Human Reproduction* (Garden City, N. Y.: Doubleday, 1970), pp. 66, 242.

5. Mark Gerzon, *The Whole World Is Watching: A Young Man Looks at Youth's Dissent* (New York: Viking Press, 1969), p. 231, n.

6. Ibid., p. 236.

7. Archibald MacLeish, "The Revolt of the Diminished Man," *Saturday Review,* June 7, 1969, p. 61. Copyright 1969 Saturday Review, Inc. Used by permission.

8. *Time* magazine, Feb. 16, 1970, p. 63.

Chapter 5.   The Underhanded Lover

1. 1 John 4:8.

2. Would it be presumptuous to suggest that I have tried to deal with such issues in an earlier work, *With Good Reason?*

3. Cf. Luke 15.

4. Genesis 1:27; cf. also Genesis 5:2.

5. Cf. Genesis 2:23-24.

6. Genesis 3:7.

7. Genesis 3:11.

8. Genesis 4:8.

9. Kurt Vonnegut's eloquently blunt comment on the absurd reality of death in any form, as in *Slaughterhouse-Five* (New York: Dell, 1971).

10. Rollo May, *Love and Will* (New York: W. W. Norton & Co., 1969), p. 218. Used by permission.

11. The first is John 13:34-35; cf. also 15:12. It should be noted here that Jesus is talking, not to the general public, but to his disciples. This is a quality of love among his avowed followers.

The second is 1 John 4:7-8, 11, 20-21. Here we must treat the author honestly, and recognize that for him "brother," "children of God," are terms referring, not to fellow human beings, but to fellow believers in Christ.

The third is probably the most famous of all, 1 Corinthians 13. In this instance, it should be noted that chapter 13 follows chapter 12—without interruption. Love is a gift of the spirit, exercised in the body of Christ.

Prelude: Love and Hope

1. 1 Corinthians 13:7, from *New English Bible, New Testament.* © The Delegates of the Oxford University Press and the Syndics of the Cambridge University Press 1961. Reprinted by permission.

2. Ibid., v. 8.

3. Ibid., v. 13.